"Now, decades after the publication of five lengthy volumes of Thomas Merton's selected letters, *A Focus on Truth: Thomas Merton's Uncensored Mind* reminds us of the wonderful, simple, direct, insightful, and frequently prophetic way Merton addressed a wide myriad of issues, along with the timelessness of his uncensored wisdom."

— Paul M. Pearson
Director, Thomas Merton Center, Bellarmine University

A Focus on Truth

Thomas Merton's Uncensored Mind

Patrick W. Collins

Foreword by
Jonathan Montaldo

LITURGICAL PRESS

Collegeville, Minnesota

www.litpress.org

Published by arrangement with Farrar, Straus and Giroux:

Excerpts from THE COURAGE FOR TRUTH: THE LETTERS OF THOMAS MERTON TO WRITERS by Thomas Merton, edited by Christine M. Bochen. Copyright © 1993 by the Merton Legacy Trust.

Excerpts from THE HIDDEN GROUND OF LOVE: THE LETTERS OF THOMAS MERTON ON RELIGIOUS EXPERIENCE AND SOCIAL CONCERNS by Thomas Merton, edited by William H. Shannon. Copyright © 1985 by the Merton Legacy Trust.

Excerpts from THE ROAD TO JOY: LETTERS TO NEW AND OLD FRIENDS by Thomas Merton, selected and edited by Robert E. Daggy. Copyright © 1989 by the Merton Legacy Trust.

Excerpts from THE SCHOOL OF CHARITY: THE LETTERS OF THOMAS MERTON ON RELIGIOUS RENEWAL AND SPIRITUAL DIRECTION by Thomas Merton, edited by Brother Patrick Hart. Copyright © 1990 by the Merton Legacy Trust.

Excerpts from WITNESS TO FREEDOM by Thomas Merton, edited by William H. Shannon. Copyright © 1994 by the Merton Legacy Trust.

1   2   3   4   5   6   7   8   9

Library of Congress Cataloging-in-Publication Data

Names: Collins, Patrick W., author.
Title: A focus on truth : Thomas Merton's uncensored mind / Patrick W. Collins.
Description: Collegeville, Minnesota : Liturgical Press, [2021] | Includes
    bibliographical references and index. | Summary: "An uncensored view of
    the life and thoughts of Thomas Merton seen through his correspondence
    with family, friends, and colleagues"— Provided by publisher.
Identifiers: LCCN 2020050444 (print) | LCCN 2020050445 (ebook) |
    ISBN 9780814688496 (paperback) | ISBN 9780814688502 (epub) |
    ISBN 9780814688502 (mobi) | ISBN 9780814688502 (pdf)
Subjects: LCSH: Merton, Thomas, 1915–1968—Correspondence. | Trappists—
    Correspondence. | Experience (Religion) | Mysticism—Catholic Church.
Classification: LCC BX4705.M542 C655 2021 (print) | LCC BX4705.M542
    (ebook) | DDC 271/.12502 [B]—dc23
LC record available at https://lccn.loc.gov/2020050444
LC ebook record available at https://lccn.loc.gov/2020050445

Contents

Foreword

Truth Matters

Thomas Merton exercised his commitments to be a writer and Christian monk by seeking "spiritual liberty." In *Conjectures of a Guilty Bystander*, he described his existential focus to live his religious life as seeking "the highest truth, unabashed by any human pressure or any collective demand." His critical public commentaries on issues of social justice, race relations, nuclear war, and interfaith dialogue were spiritual exercises to excise his writings from the "echo[es] of the 'yes' and the 'no' of state, party, corporation, army, or system" (86).

Merton as monk had discerned that efficacy in his vocation to write would depend on exercising an ability to report the singular wisdom he was continually learning in the school of his own life's more intimate relationships with God, with human cultures, and within the opportunities offered through the persons, places, and identity-transforming events of his personal history.

His desire to write and speak truth beyond his received opinions that were inculcated in him by his education, social class, and singular religious commitments, in short, his will to find his own voice, was ascetically heroic. His intuition that a grace was given to write confessing the contours of his personal struggle to be a fully integrated and truth-speaking human being was romantic. His goal to be a witness to freedom by word and example was idealized.

Competing desires within his all too human inner experiences, easily misinterpreted by his prejudices and the easiest intellectual abstractions taken, reflected the challenges to write truthfully within the complexities and personal limitations imposed by his genes and life's historical events. "Spiritual liberty," if such a human freedom actually exists for all persons by birthright, is always publicly pursued under circumstances and with language curtailed by editing and censoring. One fashions a personal truth that will be socially acceptable. Unless one is rendered unselfconscious by passing strong emotions or is drunk, no one speaks or writes publicly without the self-censorship of realizing the consequences for speaking one's mind.

For a period over two decades, from the 1940s until the mid-1960s, episcopal representatives and monks of his own Order, the Strict Cistercians, or Trappists, censored Merton's writing before publication for its conformity to church doctrine and his Order's institutional wish to reflect its popular Catholic image in America. The secular publishers and editors of his books would further modify what and how he wrote with a view to readability, to the current interests of the reading audience, and to making a profit. Merton also carefully censored himself: "I was trying to express what I thought I ought to think, and not for any especially good reason, rather than what I actually did think" (Journals, 1.4.48).

In his private journals Merton wrote to express his paradoxical "True Self," but nowhere did he speak most frankly than in his voluminous letter writing to all manner of correspondents that included church authorities, literary colleagues, social activists, and friends on a spectrum of ages and varying degrees of intimacy. No doubt that he posed for the snapshot of himself that he intuited his particular correspondent expected to see, but often he directly, in his own words, revealed dimensions of his life and thought that transcended, or went below to an inner core, the protective layers of his popular image as Catholic monk and writer. The dialogical nature of Merton's extensive conversations by mail reveals his exercising himself with spiritual liberty and free speech. His letter writing intimates his openness to having his speech and ideas challenged by those who did not share his life's commitments. He wrote letters in an uncensored voice in hopes that others would respond freely in their own voices, so that a ground of the most expansive truth between them might have an epiphany.

Editors have published five volumes of selected Merton letters from the trove of an archive well over ten thousand items. Christine M. Bochen and William H. Shannon further produced a collection from these letters grouped chronologically in general categories of the monk's personal commitments in their study *Thomas Merton: A Life in Letters*. Now Dr. Patrick Collins, a Catholic priest, teacher, writer, and musician, who for decades has studied and written on Merton's letters in articles, retreats, and sermons, gathers a portion of his studies that investigate Merton's growth in exercising freer speech in his personal correspondence. He chooses themes as diverse as "spirituality" and "ecumenism" that reveal Merton's engagements with pastoral theologies. In our time, battered by lies, half-truths, and conspiracy theories with no bases in facts, this book is timely by emphasizing Merton's urge for truth through dialogue with others that takes both correspondents beyond received opinions and what Merton called "easy answers."

I have been happy to read this portion of Father Collins's investigations into Thomas Merton's letters. For pragmatic reasons, Collins has curtailed and edited himself to meet the standards for marketability imposed by the economic realities of contemporary publishing. I await the complete harvest of his research being made available in an archive for future study by the diversely interested company of the monk's most "honorable readers." What we have in *A Focus on Truth* is only a refined, small taste of the length and breadth of Thomas Merton's journey to "spiritual freedom."

Jonathan Montaldo
The Intimate Merton: His Life from His Journals

Abbreviations

CT   *The Courage for Truth: The Letters of Thomas Merton to Writers*

HGL   *The Hidden Ground of Love: The Letters of Thomas Merton on Religious Experience and Social Concerns*

Reader   *A Thomas Merton Reader*

RJ   *The Road to Joy: The Letters of Thomas Merton to New and Old Friends*

SC   *The School of Charity: The Letters of Thomas Merton on Religious Renewal and Spiritual Direction*

WF   *Witness to Freedom: The Letters of Thomas Merton in Times of Crisis*

Introduction

The published writings of Trappist monk Thomas Merton were always censored from two sources. First, by Merton himself. He did not write all he knew, and he sometimes deleted what he had written in early drafts. He carefully selected what he considered appropriate for publication. Second, Thomas Merton was extensively censored by the Trappist Order. Merton's superiors frequently judged that things he chose to write should not be made available in print. This was not infrequently a source of great frustration to the author. In 1957, writing to Catherine de Hueck Doherty, Merton voiced his moderate and balanced concern about his Order's censorship of *The Secular Journal*. The Trappist censor had judged that some passages ". . . would shock certain readers coming from a priest, a member of this Order, and the effect of the shock would make itself felt in a harmful way . . ." He reflected to Doherty:

> My position is such that in practice I have no choice but to conform to these wishes of my Highest Superior (below the Pope) . . . I think we can certainly differ, privately and speculatively, with this opinion of censors who may not be blessed with a superabundance of judgment in such matters. Yet at the same time, they have reasons of a different order, and I think it would be rash for us to ignore these altogether. . . .
>
> My own opinion is that we ought to just drop the idea for the moment, and if God wills, we will have another chance some time later on.

So you see, the Cistercians of the Strict Observance are very much opposed to any voice with even a slightly radical sound being raised in their midst. I do not know whether or not I feel this is something for which we ought to be proud. (12.28.57 HGL 14–15)

By 1959 Merton's attitude toward this censorship neared outrage. To a woman religious correspondent, he wrote: "I can at any rate say with all simplicity that the censorship situation in our Order is utterly beyond all reason. It is an enormous penance for all concerned . . ." (Sr. M. Emmanuel, 2.3.59 HGL 181–82).

Merton's 1960s writings on social issues such as racism, nuclear weapons, war and peace, and the Vietnam War in particular intensified the censorial activities of the Order toward his more radically critical writings. In response the monk chose to be obedient—to a point. Yet he chose to mimeograph some of these articles for private circulation. They came to be called "The Cold War Letters." As he wrote in 1961 to W. H. "Ping" Ferry, "This would not require censorship" (12.21.61 HGL 20).

Merton's annoyance was expressed again in 1962 in a letter to Erich Fromm: "It takes a terribly long time to get some of it through routine censorship of the Order. Sometimes because the censor has rigid and fanatical views, and sometimes because he just can't face the possibility that a monk should be interested in a public issue. We are supposed, no doubt, to be in a permanent moral coma" (2.16.62 HGL 319).

Perhaps Merton's most extensive negative comments about the Order's censoring of his social writings were to Catherine de Hueck Doherty in 1962:

. . . the voice which was shouting, momentarily, about peace, has been told to shut up. . . . the order came in not to print or publish anything more on topics "not befitting a contemplative monk." Apparently the most crucial problems, and the struggle with the demon, these are out of range of a contemplative monk. I was told it would be all right if I prayed over these matters, however. (6.4.62 HGL 18)

By 1966 the Trappist seemed to be given more leeway by the censors as he wrote in this letter to Jean and Hildegard Goss-Mayr, colleagues in the movements for peace and non-violence:

> The practice we are following here with censorship is that the American censors do not even require to read any article except that which is submitted, on some obviously theological topic, to a big important magazine. This would not apply to any magazine of moderate circulation . . . Unless you are explicitly told otherwise by the Order, on its own initiative, you can I think simply publish anything of mine without further formalities, unless I myself say otherwise . . . (1.14.66 HGL 337)

A fuller view—and uncensored view—of the life and thoughts of Thomas Merton can be found by plumbing his correspondence with family, friends, and colleagues over the years. Five volumes of his personal and professional correspondence have been published by Farrar, Straus and Giroux. I have sought to extract from these sources many of the significant subjects about which Merton wrote, and have organized these topics chronologically. In this way readers can note the development of Merton's thoughts, feelings, intuitions, and impressions over the years on a variety of topics of concern to him. In these letters Merton was free to respond as he wished to his correspondents' questions—even though these letters were sometimes read by his abbot, Dom James Fox. As he wrote to Daniel J. Berrigan in 1963: ". . . our mail here is strictly censored and the Abbot reads it, sometimes quite carefully" (6.25.63 HGL 76).

Merton's views as expressed in his correspondence are not, of course, fully worked-out theses about any particular subjects. These letters simply express his way of dealing with particular issues at that time. And this too was, of course, conditioned by the context of the correspondent. In reading and evaluating his uncensored writings in the letters, this limitation of epistolary context must be kept in mind. On the other hand, I believe that Thomas Merton's less filtered reflections written to correspondents do say something unique and profound about the development of his life and thought. One might say of all of Merton's letters what was written by Mary Tardiff, the editor of *At Home in the World: The Letters of Thomas Merton and Rosemary Radford Ruether*: "Though these letters were never intended to be autobiographical in a formal sense, the very nature of informal letter writing lends itself to self-revelation on a personal level. Though engaged in a discussion of theological issues . . . [both writers are] disclosing profound intuitions and deeply held personal convictions" (ix).

Perhaps Merton's thoughts on the difference between the mere communication of ideas and a deeper communion of spirits between persons express something of what can be sensed through these collected letters.

> True communication on the deepest level is more than a simple sharing of ideas, conceptual knowledge, or formulated truth. The kind of communication that is necessary at this level must also be "communion": beyond the level of words, a communion in authentic experience which is shared not only on a "preverbal" level but also on a "postverbal" level. . . . And the deepest level of communication is not communication, but communion. It is wordless. It is beyond words, and it is beyond speech, and it is beyond concept." (HGL x)

It is this communion with correspondents that I hope to make available in *A Focus on Truth: Thomas Merton's Uncensored Mind.*

1

On Truth and Conscience

Thomas Merton's life could be described as an insatiable search for the truth. Whether in the secular or the sacred realms, he sought—through prayer and study—an ever clearer and more accurate experience of what is true. And that is what he expressed both in his published and private and unpublished writings. As a young man Tom Merton thought he had found truth in the Roman Catholic Church. After some reading and brief instruction in that faith tradition, he was baptized in November 1938 at the age of twenty-one. This gave him what he considered to be solid religious grounding for his considerably confused and chaotic student life.

Merton's entire life was an unending search for what is real and the true, not just in books but in living experience and practice. Truth for him was not just knowledge in the head. It was love in the heart. Therefore, he especially sought to know and experience what he later called his True Self—the God-Self within each person. Articulating truth as a writer was his life-long challenge and his great gift to the world. As he lived and as he wrote over the years, his awareness of the nature of truth developed and deepened. In *No Man Is an Island*, written in 1955, Merton expressed what he meant by truth using somewhat traditional philosophic categories. Truth is not just in what one says. Truth is who we are, he contended. Truth is ontological, nor merely epistemological. As he wrote:

> We make ourselves real by telling the truth. . . . We cannot know truth unless we ourselves are conformed to it.
> We must be true inside, true to ourselves, before we can know a truth that is outside us. But we make ourselves true inside by manifesting the truth as we see it. . . .
> What, then, is truth?
> Truth, in things, is their reality. In our minds, it is the conformity of our knowledge with the things known. In our words, it is the conformity of our words to what we think. In our conduct, it is the conformity of our acts to what we are supposed to be. (*Reader*, 120–21)

One of the chief characteristics of Thomas Merton as a person and as a writer was honesty. He wrote with great integrity of what he experienced as truth in his life. This was so true that sometimes what he wrote in later years differed from what he had written earlier. At times, in his more recent perceptions of truth, he clearly contradicted himself. This was because his view of truth was always in development through experience. Truth is perceived as always in need of purification and expansion. Merton refused to allow his experience to be a prisoner of his thoughts.

Each person, Merton judged, must be responsible toward the truth, as he wrote over and over again throughout *No Man Is an Island*:

> We are not required to manifest everything we know, for there are some things we are obliged to keep hidden from men. But there are other things that we must make known, even though others may already know them. . . .
> The seat of this deformity is in the will. Although we still may speak the truth, we are more and more losing our desire to live according to the truth. . . .
> Sincerity . . . is a simplicity of spirit which is preserved by the *will* to be true. . . .

Sincerity in the fullest sense is a divine gift . . .
. . . Life has become so easy that we think we can get along
without telling the truth. . . .
. . . Half the civilized world makes a living by telling lies.
(*Reader*, 121–22)

In the end, the problem of sincerity is a problem of love. . . .
But truth is more than an abstraction. It lives and is embodied
in men and things that are real. . . .
Our ability to be sincere with ourselves, with God, and with
other men is really proportionate to our capacity for sincere
love. And the sincerity of our love depends in large measure
upon our capacity to believe ourselves loved. (*Reader*, 125)

Thomas Merton's developing understanding of the breadth
and depth of truth can be noted in a 1963 letter that he wrote
to the psychologist Erich Fromm:

I know more and more that mere narrowly partisan positions
in religion or philosophy or anything else are simply useless
today, and I refuse to take such positions. It is the duty of man
to try to focus on the truth whatever it may be, and not to de-
ceive himself by trying to make the "truth" conform to what
keeps him happy. Of course the first truth of all is that we
cannot do this perfectly and that if we think we can we are not
going to take the first step. But surely there are better ways than
following the mass media or some approved "line" in academic
or political circles. You and I certainly agree in being dissenters
first of all, and in having much the same kind of dissent: in
favor of basically human values. Since to my mind man is made
"in God's image" it is impossible really to dissociate these
human values from the "worship" of God, and this is one of
the central truths of the Gospel. (10.8.63 HGL 321)

Truth for Christians is expressed through words because it
is a religion of the Word made flesh. There are two ways in
which persons appropriate this revealed truth: the *kataphatic*
path—through images, thoughts, concepts, and words—and

the *apophatic* path—an immediate, intuitive grasp of reality without conceptual and verbal mediation. The apophatic path into the presence of the Mystery is through silence and centering on the God within. Merton once described it as "the path that is no path" (Etta Gullick, 9.12.64 HGL 367).

In his faith journey, Thomas Merton followed both paths. He began by reading about the faith, deepening his knowledge of the reality that is essentially beyond words. As his faith matured in the monastic setting of Gethsemani Abbey, he moved more and more away from words about the Word and into the silent presence of God, which is inexpressible. This is evident in his comments about the importance and yet the limitation of Christian teaching through words.

As he entered into dialogue with persons of Eastern religious tradition, the Trappist found partners in his apophatic awareness of the limitations of words when it comes to grasping the Source of All. As he wrote to his Zen scholar friend, D. T. Suzuki, in 1959: "As you know, the problem of writing down things about Christianity is fraught with ludicrous and overwhelming difficulties. No one cares for fresh, direct and sincere intuitions of the Living Truth. Everyone is preoccupied with formulas" (4.11.59 HGL 564).

Another of Merton's correspondents in interreligious dialogue was Abdul Aziz, a Pakistani Sufi scholar and mystic. The two found themselves as Christian and Islamic with different understandings of salvation. The conceptual and verbal differences were not of primary concern to Merton, however, in 1963 when he wrote these words to Aziz:

> Personally, in matters where dogmatic beliefs differ, I think that controversy is of little value because it takes us away from the spiritual realities into the realm of words and ideas. In the realm of realities we may have a great deal in common, whereas in words there are apt to be infinite complexities and subtleties which are beyond resolution. It is, however, important, I think, to try to understand the beliefs of other religions. But much

more important is the sharing of the experience of divine light, and first of all of the light that God gives us even as the Creator and Ruler of the Universe. (6.2.63 HGL 54)

As Merton's contacts with Eastern religions and his study of these traditions expanded and deepened, and as he experimented with the contemplative practices of these great world religions, the monk moved more and more away from being principally concerned about the kataphatic expressions of faith. In apophatic contemplation, as Merton put it, "there is an underlying connection of opposites." Too great a reliance upon doctrinal formulas could lead not toward communion in the Mystery but into idolatry, as he wrote to Aziz in 1964: "I see more and more clearly that even the believers are often far short of having true faith in the Living God. The great sin remains idolatry, and there is an idolatry of *concepts* as well as of graven images. The minds of men are made vile and corrupt by the images which they worship under the pretext of 'science,' 'politics,' 'technology,' etc . . ." (12.9.64 HGL 60).

Christianity is in essence a mediated religion. The holy becomes present for people across the generations through the images and thoughts, the words and actions, of persons and events. This is what the Christian tradition calls the principle of incarnation, the sacramental principle. God disclosed the God/Self and is present in and through the human and through history. Jesus Christ is the key to this self-disclosure of presence. In him dwells the fullness of the Godhead. Through him God speaks to human beings. The Word, in this way, becomes flesh and dwells among us.

In passing on this tradition of the Word in Christianity, written narratives and verbal teachings have always been essential. The Christian Scriptures are records of God's interventions to save the world in space and time. The doctrinal teachings of the Christian community have developed from the scriptural witness in order to clarify the meanings of this mystery of salvation and to put into words just who the Word made flesh

truly is. Christianity is, in the fullest sense of the word, a religion of the Word as God's truth.

From the beginning, the words of the Bible have always
been at the heart of monastic life. *Lectio divina* and the chanting
of the Scriptures in the sevenfold Liturgy of the Hours fill the
monks' day. While Merton loved to pray and meditate on the
Word of God, he never felt himself to be a scholar of the Scriptures. In fact, in later years, he indicated a definite sense of
inadequacy in this area. During the 1960s, as the importance
of Scripture was becoming more evident at the Second Vatican
Council and in Catholic circles in general, Merton wrote to
Daniel Berrigan of the limitations of his scriptural study: ". . .
I am getting much deeper into the Bible. Frankly I have been
inhibited by the fact that for a long time there was nothing but
Catholic material on the Bible around the monastery. Now that
we have much of the best of Protestant books available, it is a
different story" (3.10.62 HGL 72).

Later in the 1960s Merton wrote to Abraham Heschel about
his biblical limitations: "I sincerely doubt my capacity to write
anything worthwhile on the Bible. I am not a pro" (12.12.66
HGL 435). And in 1967 he sought scriptural advice from his
frequent correspondent in those days, theologian Rosemary
Radford Ruether: "As to the Bible, I read it in peace and fruit-
lessly, I suppose. I don't try to follow the new stuff about it
because there is just too much. But I ought to. And since you
have mentioned that a couple of times, I wish you would rec-
ommend something" (1.29.67 HGL 500).

Systematic and moral theology are human efforts to put
God's mystery into words and logical patterns of thought.
Thomas Merton did not consider himself such a theologian in
any sense. In fact, as he wrote to Ruether in mid-February 1967:
"I distrust all academic theology. Only theology born in the
crucible of experience is any good" (Mary Tardiff, ed., *At Home
in the World*, 25). His was a spiritual or monastic theology.
While he both appreciated theologians and theologies, he saw
their limitations with regard to expressing and surrendering

to the mystery of God. This is evident in a letter to philosopher E. I. Watkin in 1962: "Even philosophically, however, I have a sneaking suspicion that what Buddhism is getting at is by no means a Platonic absolute, abstract, but right at the heart of the concrete *act of being* which is the great intuition of Thomism (not of 'the Thomists,' from whom may God deliver us). I should perhaps have said 'of St. Thomas' . . ." (11.15.62 HGL 580).

Merton's epistolary comments on moral theology are particularly interesting as they reveal his sense of the limitations of the ethics and moral theology of his time. As he wrote to Etta Gullick in 1961: ". . . as a moral theologian I am closer to Zen than to St. Alphonsus . . ." (7.25.61 HGL 344). He was always concerned about relying solely upon external authority in regard to moral choices. As he wrote to British schoolteacher John Harris in 1959, one needs also to listen to the inert authority of one's heart and conscience:

> The most difficult kind of ethic is the kind which impels you to follow what seems to be your own inner truth. And of course, you always make plenty of mistakes that way. But that is the point. I cease to understand any reason for wanting to be always right. It is so hard to do the one thing that matters, which is to be not right, but sincere. And what a difference! The Grand Inquisitors are afraid of such an approach . . . (6.22.59 HGL 392–93)

During the intense debates in the 1960s about the morality of nuclear war, Merton addressed the dead end to which traditional moral theology can lead, at times seeming to allow anti-gospel policies and actions. Again, to Harris he wrote:

> Yes, the jesuitical arguments: they present a serious problem. Especially when you apply them to something like an atomic bomb. I wonder when moral theologians are going to have to admit, finally, that things have gone so far and been blown up to such a magnitude that it is no longer humanly possible to

existentially deep within our very being. It becomes an expression of faith in God's presence.

> . . . Finally, about being united with God's will: I don't mean that you should specially formulate this in words frequently but rather just develop a habitual awareness and conviction that you are completely in His hands and His love is taking care of you in everything, that you need have no special worries about anything, past present or future, as long as you are sincerely trying to do what He seems to ask of you. . . . "When hungry eat, when tired sleep." It is basically the same attitude as the Zenists' and presupposes that one has been able to let go of useless preoccupations with oneself. And with too clear a concept of God, too, for that matter. We don't always have to cultivate the "I-Thou" stance that people make such a fuss about. When it comes in handy or is appropriate, OK.
>
> I would not be *thinking about* God's love, but just have a habitual awareness of this fact, that whether you think about it or not, everything will be taken care of, and hence what I really mean by it is not thinking about yourself and not trying to figure everything out. (2.12.66 HGL 526)

The locus of conscience is in the inner depth of a person. While the responsible Christian conscience must be formed by magisterial authority, the ultimate authority for concrete decision-making lies within the inviolable core of each person. For Merton the quality of the reflection on moral matters by external authority was a crucial matter in creating the credibility of that authority. As he wrote psychologist Erich Fromm as early as 1954:

> I fully realize the wisdom of what you have to say about types of conscience and modes of conscience formation and malformation. You can well realize that I run into all kinds of difficulties and problems, precisely where an "authoritarian" conscience is allowed to have its way. It is pitiful to see the harm that can be done in potentially fine monks by the pettiness and formalism they can get into as a result of making their

whole life depend entirely on the approval of another. (10.2.54 HGL 309)

The salvation of each person, according to Thomas Merton, is linked with following one's conscience in the ordinary matters of life. As he wrote in *The Seven Storey Mountain*, "All our salvation begins on the level of common and natural and ordinary things" (*Reader*, 87). The inevitable tensive balance between the evidences of authority and the authority of one's personal experience is detailed in a 1959 letter to John Harris. Forming one's conscience in the light of authority involves a personal appropriation of those official teachings in the light of the Holy Spirit shining from within each person. Merton shows himself in this instance to be compassionately pastoral:

> For Christ speaks in us only when we speak as men to one another and not as members of something, officials, or what have you. Though of course there are official declarations and official answers: but they never come anywhere near the kind of thing you bring up, which is personal. No one is officially saved, salvation *cannot* be that kind of thing. The other reason for not claiming to answer all your questions and solve all your problems is that I really don't think your problems are as real as they seem to be: they are indeed, or they tend to be, created by the whole false position arising out of the fact that there are so many who insist on having, and giving, official solutions. As I say, declarations can and must be made but they never get into the depths where a person finds himself in God. You may think me flippant if I say you probably believe in God already, and your problem consists not in whether or not you doubt God, but in trying to account to yourself for a belief in God which does not sound like anything official you have ever heard about this matter. And in wondering whether, that being the case, it is "the same God" you believe in.
>
> Whatever may be the intellectual aspects of the thing—I leave them to you, only suggesting that you do not have to apply yourself madly to "working" anything "out." If at the same time you can read and enjoy books by me and by Pasternak it is clear

that you are a basically religious person. And in that case, explanations and manipulations of symbols are not the most important thing but the reality of your life in God. The symbols can later take care of themselves . . . (1.31.59 HGL 385–86)

2

On Spirituality

Thomas Merton is considered by many to be one of the greatest American spiritual writers of the twentieth century. Dom Jean Leclercq ranked Merton among the early and medieval fathers of the church. Henri Nouwen spoke of him as the most important spiritual writer of the twentieth century. David Tracy suggested that Merton might turn out to be the most significant Christian figure of the century. And Lawrence Cunningham sensed that Merton, like the great patristic, spiritual theologians, could speak existentially in the language of the day about the experience of God.

Merton's greatness in the field of spirituality lies in his ability as a writer to put into contemporary terms some very ancient and traditional notions about the human spiritual journey. His was a contemplative rather than a devotional spirituality. Of the latter he wrote to Brazilian Sr. M. Emmanuel de Souza e Silva in 1955: "The Holy Spirit prays in us, in these days, with groans, *inenarrabilibus gemitibus*, as we consider the poverty and superficiality of so much that is called 'devotion'—including devotion to the Blessed Sacrament" (2.28.55 HGL 181).

The words of Merton woven into this essay are drawn from the five published volumes of his correspondence, in which

"accomplish" that reality which is beyond us—yet with us always. This is particularly the case when our intellectual study leads to spiritual dryness:

> I am more and more convinced that if you are in dryness and such, these books only increase the problem (if it is a problem).
> At the same time I think we make problems for ourselves where there really are none. There is too much conscious "spiritual life" floating around us, and we are too aware that we are supposed to get somewhere. Well, where? If you reflect, the answer turns out to be a word that is never very close to any kind of manageable reality. If that is the case, perhaps we are already in that where. In which case why do we torment ourselves looking around to verify a fact which we cannot see in any case? We should let go our hold upon our self and our will, and be in the Will in which we are. Contentment is very important, of course I mean what seems to be contentment with despair. And the worst thing of all is false optimism. (10.29.62 HGL 355)

One can have such "false optimism" if one defines and confines one's spiritual life to devotional practices. For Merton the spiritual life was above all and simply just your day-to-day life including, especially, our suffering. He expressed this to Gullick in 1963:

> As for spiritual life: what I object to about "the Spiritual Life" is the fact that it is a part, a section, set off as if it were a whole. It is an aberration to set off our "prayer" etc. from the rest of our existence, as if we were sometimes spiritual, sometimes not. As if we had to resign ourselves to feeling that the unspiritual moments were a dead loss. That is not right at all, and because it is an aberration, it causes an enormous amount of useless suffering.
> Our "life in the Spirit" is all-embracing, or should be. First it is the response of faith receiving the word of God, not only as a truth to be believed but as a gift of life to be lived in total submission and pure confidence. . . . From the moment that

I obey God in everything, where is my "spiritual life"? It is gone out the window, there is no spiritual life, only God and His word and my total response.

The problem comes when factors beyond our control make it impossible to respond in all our totality: I mean by that when a large part of our subconscious or routine or "obligatory" existence gets blocked off in such a way that it remains in opposition to, or not in union with, the will of God.

This is where you and I have to suffer much. In actual fact, if we could really let go of everything and follow the Spirit where He leads, who knows where we would be? But besides the interior exigencies of the Spirit there are also hard external facts, and they too are "God's will," but nevertheless they may mean that one is bound to a certain mediocrity and futility: that there is waste, and ineffective use of grace (bad way to talk, but you understand). The comfortable and respectable existence that you and I lead is in fact to a great degree *opposed* to the real demands of the Spirit in our lives. Yet paradoxically we are restricted and limited to this. Our acceptance of these restrictions cannot purely and simply be regarded as the ultimate obedience that is demanded of us. We cannot say that our bourgeois existence is purely and simply the "will of God." It both is and is not. . . . But we are *held back* from the deep and total gift which is not altogether possible to make in a conventional and tame setting where we do not suffer the things that the poor and disinherited and the outcast must suffer. (1.18.63 HGL 357–58)

Thomas Merton's own spiritual life, as it deepened, called him toward more solitude and silence. Later in 1963 he wrote to Etta Gullick that he was feeling torn between his external commitments and his interior life. He showed his awareness of the importance, and also the difficulty, of balancing and blending contemplation and action in all states in life:

I feel that I have to see some people, that it is a real duty, but a series of visits is really wearing because actually there is so much interior resistance to the superficial side of it and so much attraction to the real center, in interior prayer.

Obviously, anyone living a life of prayer has to confront this
kind of problem and each one has to solve it for himself in his
own circumstances. You being married obviously cannot evade
the duties of your state. I being a monk cannot nevertheless use
"the duties of my state" as a blanket pretext for avoiding all
contacts since some of them seem to be definitely willed by
God. One can never work this out perfectly satisfactorily and
therefore one always has to face the unpleasantness of a kind
of insecurity, not knowing whether one has judged rightly. But
it is a responsibility one must assume in one way or another.
Once you form your conscience to abide by God's will, you will
have all the fruits of prayer even though you may be deprived
sometimes of the enjoyment. (10.18.63 HGL 362–63)

The spiritual life involves a gradually expanding and deepening experiential awareness of God's love. As Merton would
write near the end of his life: "Our real journey in life is interior; it is a matter of growth, deepening, and of an ever greater
surrender to the creative action of love and grace in our hearts"
(Sept. 1968 RJ 118). Merton had come to realize by 1966 how
much this is true, no matter what one's spiritual "weather"
may be at any given moment. His correspondent, Etta Gullick,
apparently wrote of the purging that she had discovered to be
an inevitable and essential part of the spiritual journey. Merton
responded:

Purgations all one's life? There are no rules for that. Each one
gets what he needs, for himself or for others, and there is no
use in trying to plan on having or not having any. . . . One's
feelings can still make distinctions between consolation and
desolation, but in the depths, do such distinctions really make
much difference? Are they as real as they seem to be? As long
as desolation is real, you have to have it, and so do I. You say
you do not think you love God, and that is probably perfectly
true. But what matters is that God loves you, isn't it? If we had
to rely on *our* love where would we be? (3.8.66 HGL 375)

Thomas Merton's principal metaphor for the spiritual life
is that of journey. For him, spirituality is simply a journey from

the false self toward the True Self. During the 1960s, after having written extensively during the 1950s about the Self and the self, Merton expounded in greater and more concrete detail about what he meant. In a 1962 letter to the Pakistani spiritual scholar and seeker Abdul Aziz, Merton described the false self in terms of the exterior and interior detachments in the will:

> One must know what are the real attachments in his soul before he can effectively work against them, and one must have a detached will in order to see the truth of one's attachments. In practice, the events of life bring us face to face, in painful situations, with the places in which we are attached to our inner egoism. Exterior detachment is easier . . . But inner detachment centers around the "self," . . . in one's own will. This attachment to the self is a fertile sowing ground for seeds of blindness, and from this most of our errors proceed. I think it is necessary for us to see that God Himself works to purify us of this inner "self" that tends to resist Him and to assert itself against Him. (12.26.62 HGL 53)

As the years went by, Merton became more and more realistic and compassionate about the realities of the false self. In a letter to Etta Gullick he wrote of the false self in terms of the inevitable defects of all human character:

> As for your having defects and still knowing about the life of prayer, well, all I can say is that this is not unusual. I have never met anyone who did not have a lot of defects, and this seems to have relatively little to do with it, provided they are just things in their character which they can't really help. Such defects are very useful and do a lot for one, if one accepts them rightly. On the other hand there are a lot of defects which we could easily be without if we were not dominated by our environment, and caught as it were in a kind of trap by our own surroundings and our own history. (2.16.64 HGL 365)

This realism about the human ego and its entrapments in the environment continued to be described by Merton in a 1966 letter to Linda Sabbath. She was a young Canadian convert to

Roman Catholicism who had great spiritual curiosity, and her interests in religious experience prompted her to initiate a lengthy correspondence with the Trappist in the mid-1960s. Merton told her that no one eliminates the ego and its exterior ambiance. Rather, on the spiritual journey the ego becomes purified by the action of God cleansing us from the inside out.

> Do not attach too much importance to any individual happening or reaction, and do not look for very special significances: all is part of a purification process, with which you must be patient. You have an ego which you obviously cannot get rid of by ego-willing, and the more you try the more you will be in a bind. You cannot scheme, you cannot figure, you cannot worm your way out of it. Only God can unlock the whole business from the inside, and when He does, then everything will be simple and plain. Obviously the human element complicates everything but what else are we? Human, that's all. . . . Identify with the Ground and you won't worry too much about the weeds. The Ground doesn't. And the Ground can't be anything but Good. In Himself He plants His own seeds without you knowing or being able to do much about it. Just don't go cultivating weeds on purpose, with the idea that they are something very special, either specially good or specially bad. (3.19.66 HGL 527)

Merton philosophized in 1967 about the differing understandings of the self and the Self in Eastern and Western spiritualities. In a letter to the noted Chinese scholar John C. H. Wu, the monk pointed to the failure in the West to understand and to experience anything except the empirical "I," which is the false self. Western thought and practice find difficulty with the Eastern experience of and notion of the void as the True Self.

> At every turn, we get back to the big question, which is the question of the person as void and not as individual or empirical ego. I know of no one in the West who has treated of person in such a way as to make clear that what is most ourselves is what is least ourself, or better the other way round. It is the

void that is our personality, and not our individuality that seems to be concrete and defined and present, etc. It is what is seemingly not present, the void, that is really I. And the "I" that seems to be I is really a void. But the West is so used to identifying the person with the individual and the deeper self with the empirical self (confusing the issue by juggling around a divided "body and soul") that the basic truth is never seen. It is the Not-I that is most of all the I in each one of us. But we are completely enslaved by the illusory I that is not I, and never can be I, except in a purely fictional and social sense. And of course there is yet one more convolution in this strange dialectic: there remains to suppress the apparent division between empirical self and real or inner self. There is no such division. There is only the Void which is I, covered over by an apparent I. And when the apparent I is seen to be void it no longer needs to be rejected, *for it is I*. How wonderful it is to be alive in such a world of craziness and simplicity . . . (1.31.65 HGL 627)

Merton consistently taught that spirituality involves realizing in one's consciousness that God is ever-present in the depth of the soul. This is an experience of God which ". . . tells us *that* he is but not *what* he is. We tend to experience him as one whom we do not know" (Ripu Daman Lama, 8.16.64 HGL 453). In his 1959 letter to John Harris about the presence of God to ourselves and to all creation, he spoke of God in Zen-like fashion as a "vast emptiness" into which we sink and settle:

The great thing is not things but God Himself Who is not things but ourselves, and the world, and everything, lost in Him Who so fully IS that we come closer to Him by imagining He is not. The Being of all and my own Being is a vast emptiness containing nothing: I have but to swim in it and be carried away in it to see that this nothing is All. This too may be a distracting way of putting it: but everything is really very simple and do not let yourselves be disturbed by appearances of complication and multiplicity. *Omnia in omnibus Christus*. Let His Spirit carry you where He wills, and do not be disturbed if I sometimes talk like Eckhart . . . (5.5.59 HGL 390)

Thomas Merton's sensitivity to Eastern ways of thought and expression about the absolute Mystery can be found in a 1967 letter to his Indian poet and scholar friend, Amiya Chakravarty. Words, for Merton, were never the point. They simply pointed toward the real that is beyond yet within the human.

> The reality that is present to us and in us: call it Being, call it Atman, call it Pneuma . . . or Silence. And the simple fact that by being attentive, by learning to listen (or recovering the natural capacity to listen which cannot be learned any more than breathing), we can find ourself engulfed in such happiness that it cannot be explained: the happiness of being at one with everything in that hidden ground of Love for which there can be no explanations. (4.13.67 HGL 115)

Some Merton critics have complained that Thomas Merton was not a true theologian. Merton would have agreed—if by theology one means a systematic reflection upon the divine Mystery. Merton was, however, a spiritual theologian in the tradition of that monastic theology which expresses the human experience of God. As a gifted writer Merton was able to express with power and poetic beauty—if always, of course, inadequately—humanity's union with the divine. He wrote of his awareness of theological limitations in experiencing the Mystery to Abdul Aziz in 1963:

> Personally, in matters where dogmatic beliefs differ, I think that controversy is of little value because it takes us away from the spiritual realities into the realm of words and ideas. In the realm of realities we may have a great deal in common, whereas in words there are apt to be infinite complexities and subtleties which are beyond resolution. It is, however, important, I think, to try to understand the beliefs of other religions. But much more important is the sharing of the experience of divine light, and first of all of the light that God gives us even as the Creator and Ruler of the Universe. (6.2.63 HGL 54)

In 1965 he expressed similar thoughts to Linda Sabbath:

The only way to make any sense about the inner dimensions of religious experience is to discuss it in a framework of practice and experience. The language of science may make statements about all this, from the outside, but are such statements really relevant? Or do they simply provide certain guidelines that are useful in attempts to communicate with those who are not really interested in the real dimension?

But I am not questioning the need for an academic and technically approved approach. It has its place. (8.8.65 HGL 518)

In an extensive letter written in 1967 to Dom Francis Decroix, a Cistercian abbot of Frattocchie near Rome, Thomas Merton wrote of the ways in which contemplative theologians prefer to speak about God and theology. Implicitly he was indicating what he considered to be the limitations of both systematic and dogmatic understandings of the great Mystery.

God is not a "problem" and we who live the contemplative life have learned by experience that one cannot know God as long as one seeks to solve "the problem of God." To seek to solve the problem of God is to seek to see one's own eyes. One cannot see his own eyes because they are that with which he sees and God is the light by which we see—by which we see not a clearly defined "object" called God, but everything else in the invisible One. God is then the Seer and the Seeing, but on earth He is not seen. In heaven, He is the Seer, the Seeing and the Seen. God seeks Himself in us, and the aridity and sorrow of our heart is the sorrow of God who is not known in us, who cannot find Himself in us because we do not dare to believe or trust the incredible truth that He could live in us, and live there out of choice, out of preference. But indeed we exist solely for this, to be the place He has chosen for His presence, His manifestation in the world, His epiphany. But we make all this dark and inglorious because we fail to believe it, we refuse to believe it. It is not that we hate God, rather that we hate ourselves, despair of ourselves: if we once began to recognize, humbly but truly, the real value of our own self, we would see that this value was the sign of God in our own being . . . Fortunately, the love of our fellow man is given us as the way of realizing this. For the love of our brother, our sister, our beloved, our wife, our child, is there to see with the clarity of God Himself that we are good. It is the love of my lover, my brothers or my child that sees God in me, makes God credible to myself in me. And it is my love for my lover, my child, my brother, that enables me to show God to him or her in himself or herself. Love is the epiphany of God in our poverty. The contemplative life is then the search for peace not in an abstract exclusion of all outside reality, not in a barren negative closing of the senses upon the world, but in the openness of love. It begins with the acceptance of my own self in my poverty and my nearness to despair in order to recognize that where God is there can be no despair, and God is in me even if I despair. That nothing can change God's love for me, since my very existence is the sign that God loves me and the presence of His love creates and sustains me. Nor is there any need to understand how this can be or to explain it or to solve the problems it seems to raise. For there is in our hearts and in the very ground of our being a natural certainty which is co-extensive with our very existence: a certainty that says that insofar as we exist we are penetrated through and through with the sense and reality of God even though we may be utterly unable to believe or experience this in philosophic or even religious terms. . . .

The message of hope the contemplative offers you, then, brother, is not that you need to find your way through the jungle of language and problems that today surround God: but that whether you understand or not, God loves you, is present in you, lives in you, dwells in you, calls you, saves you, and offers you an understanding and light which are like nothing you ever found in books or heard in sermons. (8.21.67 HGL 157–58)

During the 1960s, religious experience gained intense cultural interest and became a phenomenon in the Western world. The countercultural movement of that decade sought various means to pursue parapsychological experiences of deeper realities. Drugs were sometimes used to induce such "spiritual" states. Speaking of the culture's fascination with psychedelics and mystical experiences, Merton wrote to Reza Arasteh, an Iranian born psychologist, in December of 1965: ". . . it seems to me to raise the whole question of the validity of mystical experience. And the real purpose of interior transformation by love. Love cannot be incited by a drug . . ." (12.27.65 HGL 41). Earlier in 1965 he had written to Linda Sabbath about his more personal interest in the subject of religious experience: ". . . I would have to distinguish those who do 'research in mysticism' (studying it objectively) and those who seek to deepen their own contemplative experience or that of others (subjectively and intersubjectively). I am much more acquainted with the second field" (4.25.65 HGL 517).

Later that year the Trappist engaged in a series of letters with Sabbath in which he wrote critically of this sort of self-induced psychedelic experience of transcendence:

> . . . I know my friend Zalman Schachter is quite enthusiastic about [psychedelics]. I of course cannot judge, never having had anything to do with them. However, my impression is that they are probably not all they are cracked up to be. For one thing, most of the accounts I have read or otherwise heard about seem to add up to what the Zen people call *makyo*, or the illusions that one has to put up with patiently until he gets rid of them, and things not to be taken seriously. I think that systematically induced *makyo* is hardly a good substitute for a genuine interior life, even though the latter may require one to do a little work. Theologically I suspect that the trouble with psychedelics is that we want to have interior experiences entirely on our own terms. This introduces an element of constraint and makes the freedom of pure grace impossible. Hence, religiously, I would say their value was pretty low. However, regarded merely psychologically, I am sure they have considerable interest. (12.1.65 HGL 521)

Two weeks later Merton again wrote to Sabbath in answer to her response to the above letter. He shows his sense of the limitations and shallowness of merely psychological approaches

Ought we not to distinguish between an experience which is essentially *aesthetic and natural* from an experience which is *mystical and supernatural*. I would call aesthetic and natural an experience which would be an intuitive "tasting" of the inner spirituality of our own being—or an intuition of being as such, arrived at through an intuitive awareness of our own inmost reality. This would be an experience of "oneness" within oneself and with all beings, a flash of awareness of the transcendent Reality that is within all that is real. This sort of thing "happens" to one in all sorts of ways and I see no reason why it should not be occasioned by the use of a drug. This intuition is very like the aesthetic intuition that precedes the creation of a work of art. It is like the intuition of a philosopher who rises above his concepts and their synthesis to see everything in one glance, in all its length, height, breadth and depth. It is like the intuition of a person who has participated deeply in a liturgical act. (I think you take too cavalier an attitude toward liturgy, although I confess that I am irked by liturgical enthusiasts when they want to regiment others into their way of thinking.)

By the way, though I call this experience "natural," that does not preclude its being produced by the action of God's grace (a term that must be used with care). But I mean that it is not in its mode or in its content beyond the capacities of human nature itself. Please forgive me for glibly using this distinction between natural and supernatural as if I were quite sure where the dividing line came. Of course I am not.

What would I call a *supernatural and mystical* experience, then? I speak very hesitantly, and do not claim to be an authority. What I say may be very misleading. It may be the product of subjective and sentimental illusion or it may be the product of a rationalization superimposed on the experience described above. Anyway, here goes.

It seems to me that a fully mystical experience has in its very essence some note of a direct spiritual contact of two liberties, a kind of a flash or spark which ignites an intuition of all that has been said above, plus something much more which I can only describe as "personal," in which God is known not as an "object" or as "Him up there" or "Him in everything" nor as "the All" but as—the biblical expression—I AM, or simply AM.

But what I mean is that this is not the kind of intuition that smacks of anything procurable because it is a presence of a Person and *depends* on the liberty of that Person. And lacking the element of a free gift, a free act of love on the part of Him Who comes, the experience would lose its specifically mystical quality. (11.27.58 HGL 437)

By 1965 Thomas Merton's understanding of the natural and the supernatural in mystical experience had undergone some refinement. He was by that time not so sure of some of the distinctions he had made in his 1958 letter to Huxley. As he wrote to Marco Pallis, an English scholar of Tibetan Buddhism:

Of all the questions that I treated in my last letter to you (not nearly all those which you yourself raised), the one that still bothers me is that division "natural-supernatural" in religion and mysticism. I see more and more that it is misleading and unsatisfactory, and I also think that there is every solid reason even within the framework of Catholic orthodoxy to say that all the genuine living religious traditions can and must be said to originate in God and to be revelations of Him, some more, some less. And that it makes no sense to classify some of them as "natural." There is no merely natural "revelation" of God, and there is no merely natural mysticism (a contradiction in terms). However, this whole business of natural and supernatural requires a great deal of study. The terms are not clear or unambiguous even with the Catholic tradition, always. And outside it there is a great deal of confusion as far as I can see. It is something that requires a lot of study. (Easter 1965 HGL 470)

Thomas Merton's most extensive epistolary commentary on the psychological dimensions of mystical or religious experience is found in letters to Raymond Prince, a professor of psychiatry at McGill University in Montreal and a colleague of Linda Sabbath. During the spring and winter of 1965, Prince had written to the monk about the psychological danger of regression in mysticism. Merton responded with five specific points:

1. There is certainly a great deal of mystical material which consciously and explicitly makes use of terms suggesting regression. This is especially true in Taoist mysticism, for instance. And it is true wherever mysticism is couched in terms of passivity and abandonment, which are sometimes called "quietistic," even though they might not technically earn that designation. But I think that a great deal of discrimination is needed in evaluating different accounts of mystical experience. I think in your own approach there has been a tendency to treat experiences on quite different levels more or less as if they were all on the same level.

2. It seems to me that when ecstatic experiences take on a manic character (which they sometimes do), this should be regarded as calling their authenticity into question. I do not say that this would ipso facto invalidate any such experience, but it would be an indication that caution was required, because ideally the ecstatic experience should be beyond manic excitement. There are of course diversities of temperament and personal weaknesses that have to be taken into account in each case. Very delicate problems of evaluation are involved here. In my opinion, experiences deep enough to be ecstatic or to be qualified as "unitive" should properly speaking be beyond all regressive symptoms. I would say a unitive experience that was merely regressive and narcissistic would be invalid religiously and mystically. There would be no self-transcendence, but only immersion in the self, in self-awareness as absorbed in an all which is undifferentiated. But this is not mystical union. Mystic union is not just an "oceanic feeling."

3. I think the regressive features are normal in a *transitional and early* phase of mystical development, in the so-called prayer of quiet, the night of the senses, and perhaps in

some way in the Night of the Spirit (but I question this; here at least regression must be something other than what you are talking about). I believe that regression marks these early stages because it is necessary for one to *reculer pour mieux sauter* ["to move back in order to take a better leap"]. Regression, of sorts, enables the whole self to "rest" and "return to the root" establishing a deep continuity with the past so as to enter a future that is going to demand an experience of profound rupture. (Yet there must still be spiritual continuity in spite of the rupture and rift.) The paradox is that the "old" will be left behind, and yet the "new" will be the old transformed and renewed. Death and resurrection.

4. In my opinion, attachment to the "regressive" and narcissistic peace which is proper to early and transitional stages of development is *quite usually* the reason why so few people really become mature in the mystical life. Many reach the early stage, but become bogged down in this "peace" and "sweetness" and refuse to make the break with the past which is demanded of them in order to take the leap into a "new being." I think if one simply equates mysticism with regression, a fatal error will result, and people will be encouraged not to undergo the "death" that is required in order to "live again." Of course you may say, rightly, that this "death" is a climax of regression. But it is certainly something more than narcissistic and pietistic sucking at the breast of consolation . . .

5. In my opinion, regression, the "ego" and other terms current in psychoanalysis are not strong enough to bear the weight of description required to make clear what really happens in mystical experience. A considerable deepening is going to be needed, in order to discuss these questions adequately. At least this is the opinion of one who is by no means an expert and who has barely a layman's knowledge of psychoanalysis. For one thing, the assumption

that rational and discursive knowledge is the normal peak of human intellectual and spiritual development is, to my mind, a real mistake. If we start to discuss mysticism from the viewpoint of the Cartesian cogito and the pragmatic scientific mind, we start with assumptions that make false perspectives inevitable. I think we have to restore intuitive and "direct" apprehension of reality to its proper place as a *normal* perfection of the human mind, before we can begin to understand mysticism as something that is anything but pathological. The point is that primitive people excelled, so it seems, in this intuitive and direct grasp of reality, and our development as abstract thinkers is not necessarily in all respects a genuine progress. Here again, the idea of regression takes on another (cultural) aspect. (5.22.65 HGL 493–95)

In December of 1965 Merton again wrote to Prince about the notion of psychological and spiritual regression. He compared unhealthy withdrawal from reality with going deeper into reality while admitting the danger of narcissism in the spiritual quest. He is probably keeping in mind his own experience of withdrawal to Gethsemani in 1941, his later reconnection with "reality" from his contemplative core, and then his further withdrawal into a hermitage.

First of all, returning to the question of regression in mystical experience. As I understand it, regression is a retreat from reality and is essentially narcissistic. In deeper forms of spiritual experience there is often much that resembles regression, in that one seems to "withdraw" from external reality, though I think that this is a very misleading way to conceive it, and I think that in genuine religious experience, especially mystical, one's awareness of reality is immensely heightened, the external and the interior being transcended and recaptured in a unity which is neither and both and beyond the dichotomy of subject object, inside outside and so on.

Now the problem arises: in half-baked spirituality and partial religious experience there is a tendency to substitute precisely a narcissistic unity for this transcendence. That is to say the "oceanic feeling" which is, I think, certainly regressive, and which takes the self, the superficial empirical ego self, as a kind of paradise of all being and seems to experience everything in a heightened awareness of the self (in this ego sense, not the Self of higher religions). One of the great problems of spiritual training is then to help people not to confuse this narcissistic self-awareness with true mystical contemplation. And of course people have infinite ways of getting around this. By cleverly rationalizing the narcissistic awareness in certain kinds of philosophical, psychological, theological language, for instance. Or by the language of mystical and affective love-union. (12.18.65 HGL 495)

One wonders, based upon his insights into mystical experience as expressed in his mid-1960s correspondence, how Thomas Merton would have understood and evaluated his own mystical experience in Cuba in 1939. He related this intense awareness of the nearness of heaven in *The Seven Storey Mountain*, which seems quite in line with his later thoughts on the subject, namely, mysticism as a vision of love.

It was something that made me realize, all of a sudden, not merely intellectually, but experimentally, the real uselessness of what I had been half deliberately looking for: the visions in the ceiba trees. And this experience opened another door, not a way to a kind of writing but a way into a world infinitely new, a world that was out of this world of ours entirely and which transcended it infinitely, and which was not a world, but which was God Himself. . . .

But what a thing it was, this awareness: it was so intangible, and yet it struck me like a thunderclap. It was a light that was so bright that it had no relation to any visible light . . .

And yet the thing that struck me most of all was that this light was in a certain sense "ordinary"—it was a light (and this most of all was what took my breath away) that was offered to all, to everybody, and there was nothing fancy or strange about it. It was the light of faith deepened and reduced to an extreme and sudden obviousness.

it, saying "in your heart" (aware of the place of your heart, as if the words were spoken in the very center of your being with all the sincerity you can muster): "Lord Jesus Christ Son of God have mercy on me a sinner." Just keep saying this for a while, of course with faith, and the awareness of the indwelling, etc. It is a simple form of prayer, and fundamental, and the breathing part makes it easier to keep your mind on what you are doing. That's about as far as I go with methods. After that, pray as the Spirit moves you, but of course I would say follow the Mass in a missal unless there is a good reason for doing something else, like floating suspended ten feet above the congregation.

I like the rosary, too. Because, though I am not very articulate about her, I am pretty much wound up in Our Lady, and have some Russian ideas about her too: that she is the most perfect expression of the mystery of the Wisdom of God. That is some way she is the Wisdom of God. (6.22.59 HGL 392)

From a theological perspective the Trappist wrote of prayer as grounded in the intercommunion that is the Trinity. To Etta Gullick, in 1965, he said that prayer dissolves the apparent "I"—the individual ego self—into unitive love:

What you say about the Trinity in your life of prayer is of course the most traditional thing. It is good to understand the theology of it, because when it is put into words one gets the impression that the talk is about "three objects" which one is experiencing. The ancient way of looking at it, "to the Father in the Son by the Holy Spirit," reminds us of the *unity* and the un-objective character of it. And yet they are Three, or we are in their Three and One in the Three. The authenticity of the experience depends on the dissolution of the apparent "I" that can seem to stand outside all this as subject and observe it from somewhere else. Of course we fall back into this when commenting and explaining and that is the trouble with commenting and explaining. I still think that among moderns the most authentic expression of the experience is that of the Carmelite, Elizabeth of the Trinity . . . (1.25.65 HGL 369)

In 1965 Merton wrote again to Gullick about the growing interest in prayer among people in the United States. But he questioned whether such a supposedly interior quest was well-founded. "There are a lot of people getting interested in prayer in this country, mostly in academic circles, and in a rather mixed-up context of psychoanalysis and Zen Buddhism. This is the area where people at the moment are most interested in our kind of contemplation. The Catholics are all hopped up about liturgy at the moment" (11.1.65 HGL 373).

Several times during 1965 the monk commented on intercessory prayer. It was not to him the most important sense of the prayer action or experience, it would seem. As he wrote to Dom Francis Decroix, ". . . we must be careful not to present prayer as a mere formal duty or to emphasize prayer of petition" (8.22.67 HGL 158–59). Regarding such intercession, he told Marco Pallis in 1965: "It is certainly no problem to me whatever, and never has been. I think that dealing with it might just make it more of a problem without helping those for whom it is a problem. But doubtless there would be no harm in setting down a few thoughts on the subject. I mentioned it in passing in the autobiography, but have never really dealt with the 'question' " (6.17.65 HGL 470). And to Etta Gullick, Merton wrote some very concrete advice about including specific persons and events in one's prayer.

> . . . As to intercession: let each do what he likes. Sometimes I remember a lot of people by name, other times not. . . . But obviously in one's meditation etc. one does not go dragging a lot of people in, unless it is an unusual situation. I think that in this whole question of prayer we make too many problems out of what one should do and what one should not do. These are entirely personal matters and in the same person they vary from moment to moment. The great thing is not to say that lists of names are bad or lists of names are good, but to let the person himself come to know by discernment of spirits when he should "intercede" for people by name and when not. (11.11.65 HGL 374)

How does one measure one's growth in prayer? What would constitute "progress" according to Thomas Merton? In 1965, Gullick asked him how one can judge one's progress in prayer. He warned her, in response, about the danger of too much self-focus in this matter of "measuring" one's prayer.

> Progress in Prayer: all right, if you like, I will think about writing something on it, but it is a ticklish subject because the chief obstacle to progress is too much self-awareness and to talk about "how to make progress" is a good way to make people too aware of themselves. In the long run I think progress in prayer comes from the Cross and humiliation and whatever makes us really experience our total poverty and nothingness, and also gets our mind off ourselves. But I will think a little about it. I have a real repugnance for writing things that tell everyone specifically how to do something or other spiritual now. (8.1.66 HGL 376)

Perhaps one of Thomas Merton's most profound theological reflections on prayer expressed in his published letters is contained in a 1967 letter to Dom Francis Decroix. It is thoroughly Trinitarian in its roots and focus.

> . . . we must be careful not to present prayer as a mere formal duty or to emphasize prayer of petition. We should bear in mind that Marx taught an interesting doctrine about religious alienation, which is a consequence of regarding God as distant and purely transcendent and putting all our hope for every good in the future life, not realizing God's presence to us in this life, and not realizing that prayer means contact with the deepest reality of life, our own truth in Him. Also we should perhaps point out that prayer is the truest guarantee of personal freedom. That we are most truly free in the free encounter of our hearts with God in His word and in receiving His Spirit which is the Spirit of sonship, truth and freedom. The Truth that makes us free is not merely a matter of information about God but the presence in us of a divine person by love and grace, bringing us into the intimate personal life of God as His Sons by adoption. This is the basis of all prayer and all prayer should be

oriented to this mystery of sonship in which the Spirit in us recognizes the Father. The cry of the Spirit in us, the cry of recognition that we are Sons in the Son, is the heart of our prayer and the great motive of prayer. Hence recollection is not the exclusion of material things but attentiveness to the Spirit in our inmost heart. The contemplative life should not be regarded as the exclusive prerogative of those who dwell in monastic walls. All men can seek and find this intimate awareness and awakening which is a gift of love and a vivifying touch of creative and redemptive power . . . Far from being the cause of alienation, true religion in spirit is a liberating force that helps man to find himself in God. (8.22.67 HGL 158–59)

The final words about prayer found in Thomas Merton's published letters date from January 1968. He wrote some very practical advice to Abdul Aziz about the role of reading, vocal prayer, and silence in meditation.

. . . one who is learning to meditate must also learn to get along without any support external to his own heart and the gifts of God. Hence it is good for such a one to have to remain in silence without reading or even using vocal prayers sometimes, in order to come to terms with the need for inner struggle and discipline. On the other hand this is not a universal rule. There are times when it is necessary to read, and even to read quite a lot, in order to store up material and get new perspectives. In the solitary life, however, though one has a lot of time for reading, it becomes difficult to read a great deal. One finds that in a couple of hours he reads only a few pages. The rest of the time is spent in reflection and prayer. It becomes difficult to absorb more than this. Someone in solitude who would read voraciously all the time might perhaps be considered in the wrong place. Moderate reading is, however, normal. Provided that more time is spent in prayer and meditation than in reading . . . (1.16.68 HGL 66)

Much can be learned about contemplation from Thomas Merton's uncensored writing about this subject in his published letters. Interestingly—and perhaps sadly—most of his best correspondence about contemplation is not with "official" contemplatives, like those in Holy Orders or in religious vows. It is with the laity and usually with persons who were not in the Roman Catholic community. One question that Merton addressed many times is the extent of God's call to contemplation. Is it a vocation for a few favored persons? Or are all of the baptized called to contemplation? The answer depends upon what is meant by contemplation. At times, depending upon the meaning of the word and the context of the correspondence, the Trappist says it is a special gift, and yet he also says all persons are called to contemplative living. In fact, he wrote in one place, "Christ came on earth to form contemplatives."

One of his frequent correspondents on the topic was Etta Gullick, who apparently wrote to Merton often about contemplation. In 1961 Merton seemed to judge that contemplation is not for everyone.

> I do not think strictly that contemplation should be the goal of "all devout souls," though I may have said this earlier on. In reality I think a lot of them should be very good and forget themselves in virtuous action and love and let the contemplation come in the window unheeded, so to speak. They will be contemplatives without ever really knowing it. I feel that in the monastery here those who are too keen on being contemplatives with a capital C make of contemplation an "object" from which they are eternally separated, because they are always holding it at arms' length in order to see if it is there. . . .
>
> I know what you are trying to say about loving God more than anything that exists but at the same time this is a measure of self-preservation. Beyond all is a love of God in and through all that exists. We must not hold them apart one from the other. But He must be One in all and Is. There comes a time when one loses everything, even love. Apparently. Even oneself, above all oneself. And this will take care of the rapture and all the rest because who will there be to be rapt? . . .
>
> Do collect me up in the nothingness as I do also for you. (9.9.61 HGL 345–46)

Contemplation, the Trappist contended, cannot be explained. It can only be hinted at or suggested. It is only "known" in the doing of contemplative praying and living. He wrote to Gullick in 1962 of the inadequacy of all explanatory words:

> The nothingness and emptiness are more important than their explanations, and I think you will find eventually that explanations are not needed. Yet of course you do need to communicate with someone and feel yourself understood. You are, I hope. But above all you are understood by Christ, and that is the great thing. And at the other end of it all, the least thing is to understand oneself, at least to feel that one understands himself well. (3.30.62 HGL 351)

How does one learn contemplative prayer and living? Thomas Merton says it cannot be taught. No one teaches contemplation but God. He wrote of this to Gullick in 1964:

> I do not think contemplation can be taught, but certainly an aptitude for it can be awakened. It is an aptitude which quite a lot of people might have, in seminaries and monasteries at least, as well as in any walk of life. The important thing is that this be made real and credible by someone who knows by experience what it is, and who can make it real to those in whom it begins to awaken. In a word it is a question of showing them in a mysterious way by example how to proceed. Not by the example of doing, but the example of being, and by one's attitude toward life and things.
>
> Certainly you have some sort of vocation in this regard, but you do not have to be too aware of it. Simply be content to let God use you in whatever way He wills, and be sure you do not get in his way with misplaced initiatives. (6.15.64 HGL 367)

Later in that same summer of 1964, Merton expressed himself to Gullick in terms that perhaps reflect some growing Zen influence in his understanding of contemplation: "I have greater and greater confidence in the reality of the path that is no path at all, and to see people follow it in spite of everything is comforting. By rights they should all have forgotten and lost their way long ago. If they keep on it without really knowing what it is, this is because God keeps them there" (9.12.64 HGL 367).

A few months later in 1964 the Trappist wrote to his longtime friend in New York, Catherine de Hueck Doherty, about the impossibility of "obtaining" contemplation through human efforts or techniques. Forgetting the self is the avenue to follow.

> The basic trouble is perhaps that they are still very immature in the spiritual life, because they are very centered on a "self" for which they want to attain the best of ends: they want to possess "contemplation" and "God." But to think contemplation is something that one can "attain" and "possess" is just to get off on the wrong road from the very beginning. What they really need . . . is the kind of really basic sort of training that the Desert Fathers and the early monasteries gave: to shut up and stop all their speculation and get down to living a simple laborious life in which they forget themselves. (11.21.64 HGL 22)

Contemplation is not meant to remove persons from the world. It is meant to make them ever more present to concrete, historical realities. But a contemplative becomes engaged in such external actions at a much more profound level of awareness and presence. In his first years in monastic life Merton emphasized the withdrawal from action in the world in favor of what he understood to be contemplation. But later he realized that contemplation has to be integrated into an active life. As he wrote to the Jesuit Daniel Berrigan in 1963: "I have gone through the whole gamut in this business. In the beginning I was all pro-contemplation, because I was against the kind of trivial and meaningless activism, the futile running around in circles that Superiors, including contemplative Superiors, promote at the drop of a hat" (6.25.63 HGL 78).

As Merton became more of a social activist himself during the 1960s, he wrote of the necessity—and the frustrations—of activism for one who feels called to the contemplative life. In a 1964 letter to the Shaker scholar Edward Deming Andrews, he said: "In the contemplative life one imagines that one would spend all the time absorbed in contemplation, but alas this is not the case. There are always innumerable things to be done and obstacles to getting them done, and large and small troubles" (3.13.64 HGL 39).

By 1962 Thomas Merton had clearly connected contemplation with the world of action as he wrote to his Brazilian religious friend, Sr. M. Emmanuel:

> God works in history, therefore a contemplative who has no sense of history, no sense of historical responsibility, is not a fully Christian contemplative: he is gazing at God as a static essence, or as an intellectual light, or as a nameless ground of being. But we are face to face with the Lord of History and with Christ the King and Savior, the Light of the World, who comes forth from the Father and returns to the Father. We must confront Him in the awful paradoxes of our day, in which we see that our society is being judged. And in all this we have to retain a balance and a good sense which seem to require a miracle, and yet they are the fruit of ordinary grace. In a word we have to continue to be Christians in all the full dimensions of the Gospel. (1.16.62 HGL 187)

During Vatican II, Merton feared that the Roman Catholic Church was losing its sense of rootedness in contemplation by becoming overly activistic, even in the newly emphasized active participation of the laity in the liturgy. He wrote of his fears to Etta Gullick in 1964:

> The climate of the Anglican Church seems to me to be quite favorable, especially with the background of the English school. I do honestly feel that the Anglicans have a special job to do, to keep alive this spiritual simplicity and honesty quite apart from all fuss and works. It seems to me that the atmosphere in our Church on the other hand is going to become more and more hostile to contemplative prayer. There will certainly be

official pronouncements approving it and blessing it. But in fact the movement points in the direction of activism, and an activistic concept of liturgy. I think the root of the trouble is fear and truculence, unrealized, deep down. The realization that the Church of Rome is not going to be able to maintain a grandiose and preeminent sort of position, the old prestige she has always had and the decisive say in the things of the world, to some extent even in the last centuries. Contemplation will be regarded more and more as an official "dynamo" source of inspiration and power for the big guns out there: Carmelite nuns generating spiritual electricity for the Holy Office, not so much by contemplative prayer as by action and official public prayer within an enclosure.

In a word, the temper of the Roman Church is combative and "aroused" and the emphasis on contemplation is (if there is any at all) dominated by a specific end in view so that implicitly contemplation becomes ordered to action, which is so easy in a certain type of scholastic thought, misunderstood. When this happens, the real purity of the life of prayer is gone. I must say though that there is a good proportion of contemplative prayer in the novitiate. I don't use special methods. I try to make them love the freedom and peace of being with God alone in faith and simplicity, to abolish all divisiveness and diminish all useless strain and concentration on one's own efforts and all formalism: all the nonsense of taking seriously the apparatus of an official prayer life, in the wrong way (but to love liturgy in simple faith as the place of Christ's sanctifying presence in the community). (9.12.64 HGL 367–68)

After Vatican II Merton wrote to Archbishop George Flahiff of Winnipeg, Manitoba, about his fears for the dilution of the contemplative life in monasteries in general, and at Gethsemani in particular. In the spring and again in the summer of 1966 he wrote of monasteries becoming such busy places that monks could not concentrate on the contemplative life. For him it was a matter of conscience.

I do not personally want to get involved in a great deal of very active work, but I am bound in conscience before God to say that I am deeply disturbed by the fact that I cannot ever in any way do what seems to me to be my small part, at least by discreetly participating in closed meetings, giving small retreats or occasional conferences. . . .

The basic question seems to me to be one of a *correct understanding of the contemplative life*.

My own Abbot . . . pursues what one might call a policy of negation and suppression in regard to anything that would bring monks into any kind of contact with the world . . . His view, to put it frankly, is that as long as the monks are all kept locked up in the monastery and as long as contacts of any kind with anyone outside the monastery are cut off, the monks are "contemplatives" . . .

. . . he was for a while a standing joke among the American abbots of our Order.

. . . I can say that we are not really forming contemplatives at all, that there is a great deal of unrest and questioning, and that the monks themselves feel that this kind of policy of suppression is merely stultifying and sterilizing. (5.15.66 HGL 250–52)

Thomas Merton had a long-standing dispute with Dom James Fox, his Gethsemani abbot, about not being able to travel and attend conferences outside the monastery. The abbot feared that traveling and lecturing away from the monastery would dissipate Merton's monastic energies and perhaps contribute to confusion in his vocation. To Archbishop Flahiff the monk wrote of what he felt were deleterious effects of such extreme claustration for monastics:

This principle which is being *mis*applied here is that "contemplatives" are not supposed to leave their monasteries to undertake any form of active work and this must be jealously guarded at this time since some are trying to lure them out into the active ministry. . . .

It is self-defeating and leads only to inertia and stagnation in the contemplative life. This stagnation is in fact one of the problems we confront. The stifling effect of rigid formalities is still very evident in many contemplative monasteries. . . .

The trouble with contemplative renewal is that principles can be misinterpreted and misapplied, especially in what concerns the difference between essentials and accidentals. This difference is by no means clear, and if it is so far reduced that antique customs and interpretations are still regarded as "essentials," then renewal is impossible. I would say that the whole question of communication with the outside world and information about the outside world on the part of men contemplatives (women too) is a case in point. Some are still considering that men have to be so strictly cloistered that they never go out, except in case of grave illness, never participate in study sessions, conferences, which might be of great use to them, etc. etc. Certainly there ought to be great liberality in letting them visit other monasteries, to broaden themselves. (6.7.66 HGL 253–54)

During 1967 Thomas Merton reflected with Rosemary Ruether about the secular context and the effects of contemplation upon the world. Ruether had suggested that monastic life was too anti-worldly. He contended that contemplative awareness and living leads to a less divided person because it integrates mind, soul, and body beyond the usual Western dualism. It is this unity of the person that is contemplation's great contribution to society.

I refuse in practice to accept any theory or method of contemplation that simply divides soul against body, interior against exterior, and then tries to transcend itself by pushing creatures out into the dark. What dark? As soon as the split is made, the dark is abysmal in everything, and the only way to get back into the light is to be once again a normal human being who likes to smell the flowers and look at girls if they are around, and who likes the clouds, etc. On the other hand, the real purpose of asceticism is not cutting off one's relation to created things and other people, but normalizing and healing it. The contemplative life, in my way of thinking (with Greek Fathers, etc.), is simply the restoration of man, in Christ, to the state in which he was originally intended to live. Of course this presents

problems, but I am in the line of the paradise tradition in monastic thought which is also part and parcel of the desert tradition, and is also eschatological because the monk here and now
is supposed to be living the life of the new creation in which
the right relation to all the rest of God's creatures is fully re-
stored. Hence Desert Father stories about tame lions and all
that jazz. (3.9.67 HGL 503)

In 1967 Pope Paul VI asked Thomas Merton to write something about the contemplative life for the Vatican's Synod of
Bishops. The Trappist was disturbed by the request, not knowing what, in reality, could be said. He also questioned whether
he was the best one to write on the subject of "spiritual avia-
tion." In earlier years he had had more "answers." Now he
had far more "questions" about contemplation and action.
Having become more reconnected to "the world" during the
1960s, Merton was more aware of the difficulty in conveying
the contemplative message to people of that time. He wrote of
these reactions to Dom Francis Decroix, the Cistercian abbot:

> . . . I was acutely embarrassed by the Holy Father's request.
> It puts us all in a difficult position. We are not experts in any-
> thing. There are few real contemplatives in our monasteries.
> We know nothing whatever of spiritual aviation and it would
> be the first duty of honesty to admit that fact frankly, and to
> add that we do not speak the language of modern man. . . .
> The problem of the contemplative Orders at present, in the
> presence of modern man, is a problem of great ambiguity.
> People look at us, recognize we are sincere, recognize that we
> have indeed found a certain peace, and see that there may after
> all be some worth to it: but can we convince them that this
> means anything *to them*? . . .
> When I first became a monk, yes, I was more sure of "an-
> swers." But as I grow old in the monastic life and advance
> further into solitude, I become aware that I have only begun to
> seek the questions. And what are the questions? Can man make
> sense out of his existence? Can man honestly give his life mean-
> ing merely by adopting a certain set of explanations which

pretend to tell him why the world began and where it will end, why there is evil and what is necessary for a good life? My brother, perhaps in my solitude I have become as it were an explorer for you, a searcher in realms which you are not able to visit—except perhaps in the company of your psychiatrist. I have been summoned to explore a desert area of man's heart in which explanations no longer suffice, and in which one learns that only experience counts. (8.21.67 HGL 154–56)

During the fall months of 1967, Thomas Merton commented to others about this difficult task of writing the message from contemplatives that the pope has requested. In August he admitted to Etta Gullick the importance of trying to say something about the subject:

. . . I am beginning to see that it is necessary to say some firm things about the contemplative life, and protect these people against the irresponsible gossip and nonsense of those who haven't the faintest idea what it is all about in the first place. I do hope that on your side the Anglicans will be very positive about contemplation—those who are interested. It is a matter for minorities and the majorities are all rushing off with banners waving to conquer something or other. (8.31.67 HGL 378–79)

To his friend at the Center for the Study of Democratic Institutions, W. H. Ferry, Merton was more blunt in expressing his frustrations that September. "In my private opinion the contemplatives are a bunch of dolts and squares—at least the Catholic ones, and they have nothing to say to the modern world at least until such time as they wake up and come alive" (9.5.67 HGL 234). He wrote in October in a similar vein to Bruno Paul Schlesinger, a professor at St. Mary's College in Indiana:

To me one of the most amusing things that has happened lately is this: the progressive and activist Catholics began hailing the Beatles as very hip people (which of course they are). Then all of a sudden the Beatles start going to a yogi to learn contemplation—which is anathema to the progressive etc. Catholics. Hm. My feeling is that our progressives don't know what they are talking about, in their declarations about modern man, the modern world, etc. Perhaps they are dealing with some private myth or other. That is their affair . . . (10.16.67 HGL 546)

For the Trappist, contemplatives were not without hope for the future, however. With his ever-broadening reading and learning from persons in other cultures, Thomas Merton found the greatest hope for the future of the contemplative life in the Third World. In September of 1967 he wrote to an African priest, later a Tanzanian bishop, named Christopher Mwoleka, stating that the African sense of the wholeness and unity of life could give a new birth to the contemplative life:

. . . I believe that African Christians will bring new life to the Church of the future. Perhaps God wants you to experience contemplation in a deeply African way, which I would surmise to be a way of wholeness, a way of unity with all life, a sense of the deep rhythm of natural and cosmic life as the manifestation of God's creative power: and also a great warmth of love and praise. If you realize that God has indeed given you His Spirit as the source of all joy and strength, and trust Him to purify your heart with His presence and love, in great simplicity, He will teach you the joy of being a child of God, an African child of God with your own special unique gifts. (9.13.67 HGL 462)

3

On Liturgical Renewal

The first and most obvious effect of Vatican II was the reform and renewal of the worship life of the church. Liturgical change dramatically affected every Catholic community in the world. The Constitution on the Sacred Liturgy, promulgated on December 10, 1963, began the first radical reform of the structures of Roman Catholic liturgical life since the Council of Trent reformed the liturgy with the Missal of Pope Paul V in 1570.

Thomas Merton's first adult experience of Roman Catholic worship occurred while he was studying at Columbia University in New York City. One Sunday morning he felt an urge to attend a Roman Catholic Mass, and so he walked into nearby Corpus Christi Church. He was deeply impressed by the serious prayerfulness of those attending the Masses there, as he recorded in his autobiography:

> What a revelation it was to discover so many ordinary people in a place together, more conscious of God than of one another; not there to show off their hats or their clothes, but to pray, or at least to fulfill a religious obligation, not a human one. For even those who might have been there for no better motive than that they were obliged to be, were at least free from any of the self-conscious and human constraint which is never ab-

sent from a Protestant church, where people are definitely gath-
ered together as people, as neighbors, and always have at least
half an eye for one another, if not all of both eyes. (*Seven Storey
Mountain*, in *Reader*, 91)

During the Mass Merton was moved by the "clear and solid
doctrine" that was preached that day, "for behind those words
you felt the full force not only of Scripture but of centuries of
a unified and continuous and consistent tradition. And above
all, it was a vital tradition: there was nothing studied or antique
about it" (*Reader*, 92). He left liturgy at the end of what was
then called the Mass of the Catechumens, and as he walked
leisurely down Broadway in the sun: "All I know is that I
walked in a new world" (*Reader*, 94).

Thomas Merton was baptized as a Roman Catholic at Corpus Christi Church on November 16, 1938. In his early years
as a Catholic, he experienced the importance of the liturgy in
his own life and participated in Mass as often as possible—
often every day. In 1949, after eight years in the monastery, he
wrote to his Columbia University friend, Robert Lax, of his
deep sense of Scripture and the liturgy:

> Someone should be able to find the living God in Scripture—
> and this is His word—and then lead others to find him there,
> and all theology properly ends in contemplation and love and
> union with God—not ideas about Him and a set of rules about
> how to wear your hat. The Mass is the center of everything and
> in so far as it is Calvary it is the center of Scripture and the key
> to everything—history, everything. All the trouble going on
> now. (11.27.49 RJ 172)

Merton's early reactions to the liturgical reforms of Vatican II
were largely negative. He had come to love the Latin prayers
and chants of the pre–Vatican II liturgy during his twenty-five
years as a Catholic. As an intellectual, Merton had a solid
knowledge of Latin. He found it most effective to pray the
liturgy in that traditional ritual language. These rich traditions,

he feared, were being replaced after the council with overly enthusiastic experimentations, which he judged to be trite and banal.

Liturgical music was one of the first things to change. Music in the vernacular for congregational participation began to be borrowed from the Protestant tradition. Some vernacular music was also being composed by Catholics. By 1964 the Trappist felt it to be an experience of musical impoverishment: "I passed your English-Gregorian texts to our choirmaster, who is a little cool toward Gregorian with English as I am myself. But I am not as cool as he is because I am no professional, and as far as I am concerned I think people ought to try out everything feasible and see what happens. The texts look all right but not inspiring to me" (Leslie Dewart, 9.23.64 WF 298).

Merton's lack of enthusiasm for liturgical reform, rooted in his love and respect for tradition, had been expressed prior to the council in a letter to his former Gethsemani novice, the Nicaraguan priest-poet Ernesto Cardenal: "The psalms are for poor men, or solitary men, or men who suffer: not for liturgical enthusiasts in a comfortable, well-heated choir" (11.18.59 CT 120).

As the council began in October of 1962, the first topic for discussion was liturgy. Merton reacted to these early conciliar discussions with cautious hope in a letter to his English correspondent, Etta Gullick: "Apparently they are on the liturgy now. I don't know what will come, but the whole thing seems to be making sense. Probably it is bound to bog down a bit somewhere, but it is going better than expected" (10.29.62 HGL 355).

By December 1963, following the promulgation of the Constitution on the Sacred Liturgy, the first solemn declaration of Vatican II, Merton was less optimistic in his letter to the philosopher E. I. Watkin:

> The question of liturgy is of course a very complex one, and I think it is going to disturb very many people on both sides of

the question. The adaptation is not going to be easy, nor is the sweeping optimism of liturgical reformers always a guarantee of the greatest intelligence. I am afraid that inevitably much that is good will be lost, and needlessly lost, and this will be very sad . . . However, it is certain that there must be a warmer and more intelligent relationship between what goes on at the altar and what is done by the people. It is easy enough for you and for me to appreciate the familiar forms which have remained to a great extent unchanged since Charlemagne. It is also easy for us to understand the Middle Ages and to feel our deep indebtedness to them, and to realize the continuity of our experience with that of the Middle Ages. A vast majority of Christians in our day cannot do this, unfortunately . . .

. . . I recognize the justice of your remarks on the liturgical paper and hasten to add that I am not much of a "liturgist" in the modern and fashionable sense, and really at heart I agree with you, for myself. I am very content with the simple Cistercian liturgy we have, and hate to think that it may be suddenly and violently wrenched out of shape for no particularly good reason, as the needs of a monastery are not those of a parish. But the obsession with the latest "thing" is so strong that even monks get swept away by it. And I am heartily in agreement with you in deploring this. (12.12.63 HGL 584–85)

From the start, the Trappist had found fault with the dominant approach to liturgical reform that seemed to favor haste over caution. Merton's negative reactions to the rapid and enthusiastic changes were rooted in many sources. Principally he feared that the contemplative dimension of public worship was being undermined through an overly activist approach. To Gullick in March 1963, he wrote: ". . . I don't hold with these extreme liturgy people for whom all personal and contemplative prayer is suspect. If you make a meditation they think you are a Buddhist" (3.24.63 HGL 359).

Thomas Merton had been studying Buddhism for some time. He had found the Zen approach to meditation to be very helpful for his own prayer and worship. To E. I. Watkin he had written in November 1962:

That brings me to Buddhism. I am on and off thinking a great deal about it, when I can, because I think in many ways it is very germane and close to our own approaches to inner truth in Christ. Naturally, I am glad to find myself in the company of such a man as Don Chapman, in being called a Buddhist, because that is one of the standard jokes in the community here: that I am a hermit and a Buddhist and that in choir I am praying as a Buddhist (how do they know?), while others are all wrapped up in the liturgical movement and in getting the choir on pitch and in manifesting togetherness, whatever that is. Really I do not feel myself in opposition with anyone or with any form of spirituality, because I no longer think in such terms at all: this spirituality is *the* right kind, that is *the* wrong kind, etc. Right sort and wrong sort: these are sources of delusion in the spiritual life and there precisely is where the Buddhists score, for they bypass all that. Neither this side of the stream nor on the other side: yet one must cross the stream and throw away the boat, before seeing that the stream wasn't there. (11.15.62 HGL 580)

By 1964, Merton's fears about the loss of the contemplative dimension in liturgy were deepening. He wrote to Gullick:

It seems to me that the atmosphere in our Church . . . is going to become more and more hostile to contemplative prayer. There will certainly be official pronouncements approving it and blessing it. But in fact the movement points in the direction of activism, and an activistic concept of liturgy. I think the root of the trouble is fear and truculence, unrealized, deep down. . . .

In a word, the temper of the Roman Church is combative and "aroused" and the emphasis on contemplation is (if there is any at all) dominated by a specific end in view so that implicitly contemplation becomes ordered to action, which is so easy in a certain type of scholastic thought, misunderstood. When this happens, the real purity of the life of prayer is gone. I must say though that there is a good proportion of contemplative prayer in the novitiate. I don't use special methods. I try to make them love the freedom and peace of being with God alone in faith and simplicity, to abolish all divisiveness and diminish all useless strain and concentration on one's own efforts and all formalism: all the nonsense of taking seriously the apparatus of an official prayer life, in the wrong way (but to love liturgy in simple faith as the place of Christ's sanctifying presence in the community). (9.12.64 HGL 368)

Merton also feared that the beauty of ritual language would not be respected in the translations of the liturgical texts. He wrote of this to his Oxford scholar and Anglican friend, A. M. Allchin, in April 1964:

I do think it is terribly important for Roman Catholics now plunging into the vernacular to have some sense of the Anglican tradition. This, however, is only a faint hope in my own mind, because on the one hand so many of the highest Anglicans are outrageously Latin, and on the other the beauty of the *Book of Common Prayer*, etc., is out of reach of the majority in this country now, and is perhaps no longer relevant. But the spirit and lingo of modern Roman Catholicism in English-speaking countries has been in so many ways a disaster! (4.25.64 HGL 26)

By the fall of 1964, Merton expressed some tentative views of liturgical renewal in his own monastic community, as he wrote to philosopher Leslie Dewart:

Actually, however, this liturgy thing has, at least in monasteries, become so much of a professional specialty that I am not one of those that can afford initiatives and declarations. I go along with it, and enjoy what is offered, but I cannot do the offering (of new texts and ideas) though people have pestered me a little to write hymns and whatnot. I don't intend to touch any of it because I think it is all extremely fluid (as it ought to be) and the flowing is usually a mile ahead of me, as I cannot keep up with the required information, attend conferences, and so on. It would be naive of me to try to contribute anything worthwhile. I have a rather silly article on liturgy coming out in the Critic in December, but that is only a gesture of good will. (9.23.64 WF 298)

By 1965, Merton's fears about the loss of liturgy's contemplative core were being confirmed by his own and others' liturgical experiences. He was also more and more aware of his
own inadequacy in the area of liturgical history and the imple-
mentation of the reforms. Later that year Merton noted with
appreciation that there was a growing interest in prayer and
contemplation throughout the world. But liturgy was of little
help in this regard, as he wrote to Gullick: "There are a lot of
people getting interested in prayer in this country, mostly in
academic circles, and in a rather mixed-up context of psychoanalysis and Zen Buddhism. This is the area where people at
the moment are most interested in our kind of contemplation.
The Catholics are all hopped up about liturgy at the moment"
(11.1.65 HGL 373).

By 1967, Thomas Merton was expressing more positive
views of liturgical renewal. He seemed to sense more gain than
loss in the changes in worship. This was clearly a change from
his earlier attitudes. In his letter to friends at Pentecost, he
expressed what the liturgical reforms had come to mean to
him personally. He also noted that there were considerable
positive results in the worship life of parishes.

> Personally, my own life and vocation have their own peculiar
> dimension which is a little different from all this. I have always
> tended more toward a deepening of faith in solitude, a "desert"
> and "wilderness" existence in which one does not seek special
> experiences. But I concur with these others in being unable to
> remain satisfied with a formal and exterior kind of religion.
> Nor do I think that a more lively liturgy is enough. Worship
> and belief have become ossified and rigid, and so has the reli-
> gious life in many cases.
>
> Certainly it is fine that now the liturgy is becoming more
> spontaneous, more alive, and people are putting their hearts
> into it more. (I am not saying it was not possible to enter into
> the old Latin liturgy, but it was hard for many.) But we need a
> real deepening of life in every area . . . ("Circular Letter to
> Friends," Pentecost 1967 RJ 102–3)

That concern for "depth" and Merton's more balanced view of liturgical reform was expressed again in the fall of 1967 in his letter to a woman religious:

> . . . I am sure that the basic thing will always remain the need for deep prayer in the heart, and the deepest and most authentic response to the word of God. We must certainly bring renewal to our liturgical worship, but we must also preserve a place for silence and for contemplative prayer. However, it must be admitted that entirely new ways of explaining contemplative experiences must be found. However, when we see the Beatles (you've heard of them in England?) going to an Indian Yogi to learn meditation, it can certainly not be said that all desire for the contemplative life is extinct in modern youth!!! (Sr. Maria Blanca Olim, 10.16.67 WF 198)

By December of 1967, the Trappist had celebrated some small group liturgies which gave him an even more positive attitude about some of the directions of liturgical renewal. He expressed this in a letter to author John Howard Griffin:

> I just got through a really marvelous new venture: first time a group of cloistered nun-superiors was here for retreat and seminar, fifteen of them, including your "neighbor," Mother Henry of the cloistered Dominicans at Lufkin. We had a really first-rate session, ending with Mass together at the hermitage yesterday, and such a Mass as you never saw: all joined in to give bits of the homily, to utter petitions at the prayer of the people, etc. etc. Really groovy, as they say. (12.8.67 RJ 139)

The old adage "experience is the best teacher" proved to be true for Merton and the reformed liturgical rites. Before his death in 1968, the Trappist had come to appreciate much of the new approaches, although he remained somewhat skeptical of liturgical experiments. As he wrote to a high school student correspondent in April 1968:

> Good folk music at Mass can be a big help, but bad singing and trifling hymns are not much help. But so is bad Gregorian an

all seemed quite simple to him. One just listened and obeyed. But as his experience of monastic life and the church evolved, the Trappist formed some serious questions about both the effectiveness and the wisdom of authority as it was being exercised. This brought him into a crisis of conscience about the meaning and extent of obedience—both for himself and for those with whom he corresponded.

Most of the published letters quoted in this section were written during or in the wake of Vatican II. The ecumenical council had grounded the church in a quite different approach to authority and freedom through the collegial experiences of that council, and the conciliar documents that called for collegiality throughout the church.

As always, the Trappist could see the light and the dark in the many proposals for change. In a letter to Mother Myriam Dardenne in March 1965, Merton elaborated his thoughts on freedom in light of what he considered to be the overly enthusiastic attitudes and actions of postconciliar reformers:

> I find the naive approach to these things a bit irritating at times, because in reality it seems to me that the problems of the Church and of our Order are quite serious and profound. The chief problem is that of freedom of the spirit, and allowing the Christian to develop and grow, rather than keeping him in a straitjacket forever. On the other hand, of course, so many people desire control and though they do not even admit this, they fear freedom and want to be told what to do all the time, provided that they can sometimes have the pleasure of resisting and attracting the attention of authority. And of criticizing others who do not absolutely conform. (3.6.65 SC 268)

As Merton grew in monastic life, he chose not to conform in many ways. He judged that monks were reluctant to let go of the external authoritative norm and launch out into the deep with the Holy Spirit, who knows how to resolve contradictions a lot better than the Holy Office, which seems to exist in order to maintain official norms. A healthy and dialogical understanding of and practice of authority was what the Trappist was convinced was needed. In 1963 he wrote to philosopher Leslie Dewart, describing what he felt to be the stultifying effect of authority and obedience as practiced both in the church and in his religious Order:

> The situation regarding authority and so on is very complex. It is not by any means that a lot of conservative Superiors are standing in the way of enlightened subjects. The whole concept and practice of religious obedience has stultified the clergy and the religious, so that they are incapable of any creative action, and equipped only to run in one familiar organizational groove. The way we are now, the Church is simply incapable of genuine adaptation. In a word, if the Council doesn't continue waking up the Bishops and Superiors, we are going to be in a bad way.
>
> This is not conclusive, and it is all from the top of my head. More of the old pessimism, and I don't mean it to be as bad as it probably sounds. I am just wondering. Where do we look for something genuinely positive? (5.10.63 WF 287)

In 1965 Thomas Merton wrote to his friend in Santa Barbara, W. H. Ferry, of his concerns regarding the inadequacy of superiors in the church. This was in response to a proposal to establish a priests' union in order to deal with the injustices of superiors toward priests.

> . . . even in the Council it was spelled out that the relations with ecclesiastical Superiors were not what they should be, and it was also said, in traditional terms, that the Superiors ought to get down to the business of mending their ways. The trouble is of course that they can't. They don't see the problems the way subjects do, especially if they have been in a Chancery Office for years, twenty, thirty, forty, some of them. And think of those characters who have been in the Vatican since they were teenagers practically. They just have no idea what the score is, and they don't know how to look squarely at the problems of subjects, especially they do not and cannot understand the difference between the real problems of creative initiative

and the neurotic kid problems that, in fact, they generate in subjects and unconsciously like to perpetuate. The relations of Superiors and subjects, in religion and in the secular clergy, are very often completely puerile, centered on artificial and illusory problems which are almost deliberately kept going because they create an illusion of important decisions being made. All this nonsense could be avoided with a minimum of maturity.

. . . the Superiors are never going to solve it themselves. On the other hand, the Superiors respond only to pressure. And we cannot get higher Superiors to bring pressure on lower Superiors, they are all in cahoots like a gang of thieves, and all support one another in tricky procedures, secret power plays, cheating, etc. etc. Hence the only thing to do is to bring pressure from the secular arm so to speak. . . .

In my opinion, I think that the risks of this approach should be studied objectively. . . . Personally, I think that it will do a great deal of harm to the Church, if it is not handled with extreme tact and care . . . But I think nevertheless, theologically and biblically, we have to ascertain whether the Church is the kind of body that can stand such a thing as a priest's union without getting into schism. I think that the fact that they start out uncritically making no distinction between a labor union and a "priest's union" shows that there is danger of being wrong from the beginning, because, however you look at it, the relation of a priest to his bishop is not that of an employee to an employer. Hence the problems that arise between them, and the very real question of the priest's rights, need to be expressed in a different form. . . .

My frank opinion on this is that instead of forming a priests' union and causing public pressure with a lot of noise in the press, priests should form a kind of private association for settling their problems in the more or less "regular" way, and it would be understood that instead of appealing to outside pressure they would make it understood that if they continued to get the runaround they would simply get out, get secularized, and use their talents in some other way where they would be less obstructed. The need of priests is considerable these days, but is presented in artificial statistical sort of language which is really bypassing all issues. Yet it scares the bishops. If they realize that they are just not going to have any decent priests

left, and that they will be stuck with aged cranks, creeps,
seventy-year-old infants and so on . . . they may think things
over. (1.26.66 HGL 223–25)

Two months later Merton continued in the same vein, with
regard to Fr. William DuBay, a priest of the Archdiocese of Los
Angeles, who was proposing such unions:

> . . . the kind of collision course with authority that he advo-
> cates is not going to get anywhere really. The whole situation
> is already so vitiated with politics that his ideas will only make
> it ultra-political. The whole source of the authority problem in
> the Church is precisely that Superiors act too much as politi-
> cians and manipulate subjects for purely institutional ends. Du
> Bay's course seems to point to an even worse kind of institu-
> tionalism in the long run. (W. H. Ferry, 3.11.66 HGL 225)

Monk Merton expanded on his sense of the limitations and
wrongheadedness of religious authority in his Septuagesima
Sunday "Circular Letter to Friends" in 1967. His extended
comments were stimulated by the decision of the prominent
English theologian and writer Charles Davis to resign from
both the priesthood and the Roman Catholic Church. While
Merton sympathized with Davis's reasons for leaving insofar
as they related to authority issues, and while he respected
Davis's choice, Merton gave his reasons for remaining in the
church despite the many acknowledged and serious ecclesiastical difficulties.

> There has been a lot of talk about Fr. Charles Davis and his
> farewell to the Church. Note, his problem was Church author-
> ity, not celibacy. He could conceivably have left the priesthood
> and got married with a dispensation. In a long statement which
> was front page news in England, he made some very drastic
> criticisms of the abuse of authority in the Church. I do not think
> these criticisms were altogether baseless or unjust. The present
> institutional structure of the Church is certainly too antiquated,
> too baroque, and is so often in practice unjust, inhuman, arbi-
> trary and even absurd in its functioning. It sometimes imposes

useless and intolerable burdens on the human person and demands outrageous sacrifices, often with no better result than to maintain a rigid system in its rigidity and to keep the same abuses established, one might think, until kingdom come. I certainly respect Fr. Davis's anguish—who of us does not sometimes share it? But I cannot follow him in his conclusion that the institutional Church has now reached the point where it can hardly be anything other than dishonest, tyrannical, mendacious and inhuman. He feels he has a moral obligation to leave the Church and he offers this theological justification for his decision.

I hope most of us Catholics have learned by now that this kind of decision on the part of one of our brothers merits our compassion and understanding, not fulminations against heresy and bad faith. One can feel Fr. Davis is still a brother without coming to the same conclusions as he did. . . .

. . . At times one wonders if a certain combativeness is not endemic in Catholicism: a "compulsion to be always right" and to prove the adversary wrong. A compulsion which easily leads to witch-hunting and which, when turned the wrong way, hunts its witches in the Church herself and finally needs to find them in Rome. There are always human failures which can be exploited for this purpose. . . .

There comes a time when it is no longer important to prove one's point, but simply to live, to surrender to God and to love. There have been bad days when I might have considered doing what Fr. Davis has done. In actual fact I have never seriously considered leaving the Church, and though the question of leaving the monastic state *has* presented itself, I was not able to take it seriously for more than five or ten minutes. It is true that if I had at one time or other left the Church, I would have found scores of friends who would have approved my action and declared it honest and courageous. I do not claim any special merit in having decided otherwise. Nor does a decision for Christian obedience imply an admission that I think authority has always been infallibly just, reasonable or human. Being a Catholic and being a monk have not always been easy. But I know that I owe too much to the Church and to Christ for me to be able to take these other things seriously. The absurdity, the prejudice, the rigidity and unreasonableness one encounters in some Catholics are nothing whatever when placed in the balance with the grace, love and infinite mercy of Christ in His Church. And after all, am I not arrogant too? Am I not unreasonable, unfair, demanding, suspicious and often quite arbitrary in my dealings with others? The point is not just "who is right?" but "judge not" and "forgive one another" and "bear one another's burdens." This by no means implies passive obsequiousness and blind obedience, but a willingness to listen, to be patient, and to keep working to help the Church change and renew herself from within. This is our task. Therefore by God's grace I remain a Catholic, a monk and a hermit. I have made commitments which are unconditional and cannot be taken back. I do not regard this position as especially courageous: it is just the ordinary stuff of life, the acceptance of limits which we must all accept in one way or another: the acceptance of a sphere in which one is called to love, trust and believe and pray—and meet those whom one is destined to meet and love. . . .

More and more since living alone I have wanted to stop fighting, and arguing, and proclaiming and criticizing. I think the points on which protest has been demanded of me and given by me are now well enough known. Obviously there may be other such situations in the future. . . . When one gets older (Jan. 31 is my fifty-second birthday) one realizes the futility of a life wasted in argument when it should be given entirely to love. (Septuagesima Sunday 1967 RJ 95–96)

A few months later Thomas Merton had occasion to write about his views on conscience and obedience in response to a letter from Daniel Berrigan. The Jesuit social activist was about to be disciplined by his religious superiors for his participation in social protests, and Berrigan had sought Merton's counsel. In response the Trappist vented some of his own frustrations and even anger with his superiors.

The one real clear thought I have is that obviously sooner or later it is going to be a question of obeying God or obeying man. Do they really have the right to forbid you to follow your conscience in this? Sooner or later they reach the point where they think they have to cut you down in favor of their institutional view of the Church. And you can't accept. Maybe this is the time. But are there any questions and reservations? . . .

In short, Dan, if you think this is it, then go ahead. And let them heave you out. And don't worry about the consequences: but just watch yourself in the mushroom cloud that follows, be sure in all things you are really trying to do it in God's way as a real Jesuit (because sometimes the real ones are the ones on the outside of organizations). (4.15.67 HGL 94)

Earlier, in 1966, the Trappist had spoken of the coming crisis of obedience and authority in the church in another letter to Berrigan:

. . . I would say don't needlessly get involved in big symbolic confrontations. Later, however, such things may arise. I say later because I think of the big explosion of the obedience-authority crisis that is sure to come. . . .

What is demanded is a real renewal, not just an explosion. . . .

The moment of truth will come when you will have to resist the arbitrary and reactionary use of authority in order to save the real concept of authority and obedience, in the line of renewal. This will take charismatic grace. And it is not easy to know when one is acting "charismatically" when one is surrounded with a great deal of popular support on one side and nonsensical opposition on the other. . . .

. . . let us work for the Church and for people, not for ideas and programs. (2.14.66 HGL 90–91)

In his Pentecost 1966 "Circular Letter to Friends," Merton expressed with great clarity his sense of the need for greater freedom within the church. This again reflected the movement toward collegiality and freedom taught by Vatican II that was being implemented at that time: ". . . everyone is looking for a less systematic and less rigid kind of Church structure, something that leaves room for a more charismatic kind of religion, and this gave some of us a small glimmer of hope." He personally sought more depth and more liberty within the church.

> There is everywhere a kind of hunger for the grace and light of the Spirit in forms that can be actually *experienced*. . . . I have always tended more toward a deepening of faith in solitude, a "desert" and "wilderness" existence in which one does not seek special experiences. But I concur with these others in being unable to remain satisfied with a formal and exterior kind of religion. Nor do I think that a more lively liturgy is enough. Worship and belief have become ossified and rigid, and so has the religious life in many cases. The idea that "the Church" does all your thinking, feeling, willing, and experiencing for you is, to my mind, carried too far. It leads to alienation. After all, the Church is made up of living and loving human beings: if they all act and feel like robots, the Church can't experience and love in their behalf. The whole thing becomes an abstraction. . . . But we need a real deepening of life in every area, and that is why it is proper than laypeople and others who have been kept in subordinate positions are now claiming the right to make decisions in what concerns their own lives. This is also true in religious orders. As long as everything is decided at the top, and received passively by those at the bottom, the vocation crisis will continue. There is no longer any place in our life for a passive and inert religiosity in which one simply takes orders and lets someone else do all the thinking. Those who fail to accept such a situation are not rebels, most of the time, they are sensitive and intelligent human beings who protest against a real disorder and who have a right to be heard. (RJ 102)

Despite his deep desire for freedom within the church and his Order, Thomas Merton always understood the need for structure and law and so could not be called an antinomian. His respect for the canon law that orders church life is reflected in two letters to John Harris, who was seeking an annulment of his marriage. Merton, on the other hand, also indicates his awareness of the limitations of the law when it comes to spiritual matters especially.

. . . I haven't the faintest understanding of the marriage red
tape that the Church has brought into existence, and any advice
I could give you would probably only make matters much
worse. You will have learned all about the ins and outs of the
case, and whether or not you are a candidate for what is (seriously too) called the "Pauline privilege." I always double up
with laughter at the symbolic slips which the canonists can
make with straight faces. After all the interminable talk about
the sacredness of marriage, there is the equally straight-faced
and "so-obvious" readiness to call it a privilege to get out of
the sacred bond. "Well, why didn't you say that in the first place
. . . etc. etc."

The best I can say is, be patient: God is not bound by the
stupidity of theologians and canonists . . . (5.5.59 HGL 388)

After such critical comments, Merton showed a pastoral
sensitivity and balance in the same letter to Harris as he discussed the reciprocal relationship between law and liberty in
the church:

The great consolation that no one can take away from us is that
we are Christians, that we have died with Christ and risen with
Him and are free men, and that we not only have "privileges"
which permit us to get away with little things here and there,
through loopholes in the law—we are obliged by our Christian
calling to be "no longer under the Law." This does not mean
Antinomianism. The outlaw just runs away from the Law: he
is temporarily out of reach of the Law. With us, not so. But there
comes the equal obligation of being patient with the Law—and
patience is possible insofar as we are above it, by Love. The
trouble with those who have to struggle with the Law is that
they want only something negative, to be without the Law. But
what we want is a higher and perfect law, which is Love—the
freedom of the sons of God. That is our highest obligation. Forgive the sermon . . . Do please remember that you are married,
there is no question of it in the sight of God, in your hearts. This
other business is part of the exterior routine that unfortunately
goes with Church life. But the sacraments are so great and the

Life that is in them so vast that a little patience with these externals is worth it in the long run. (5.5.59 HGL 388–89)

A few weeks later Merton wrote again to Harris, speaking once again rather disparagingly as well as humorously about canonists and annulments: ". . . if they set their minds to it, the lawyers can do anything. After all they live in a purely fictitious universe, so since it is of their own making, they ought to be able to do what they like with it, with a little dogged patience and humorlessness" (6.22.59 HGL 391).

Merton had another occasion to offer pastoral comments on the important role of law and the liberty of conscience in a letter to his aunt, Elsie Jenkins, in June 1965:

> As time goes on, we are beginning to see that all these marriage problems . . . are not necessarily the final word on how one stands with God. The Church bureaucracy has made things much too complex. I hope that soon things will be ironed out so that such difficulties will arise more seldom . . . but I think it is one which you can take up in all simplicity before God and trust in Him. Try to do what is right, as best you can, and everything will work out ok, even though from the human and institutional viewpoint everything may not be quite perfect. If we all had to do things just in the way that suits the Roman Curia, I think we would find life a lot more complicated than it should be, or that Our Lord intended it to be. Of course if you do get a chance to fix things officially with the Church, take it. (6.16.65 RJ 72)

Monk Merton's attitude to the Vatican bureaucracy could perhaps best be expressed in the phrase, "Spare me!" As he wrote to his Oxford Anglican colleague A. M. Allchin in 1965: "I would love to be ordered somewhere via Oxford, and might even consent to go to Rome if I thought I could go via Oxford, but hardly otherwise. . . . It is the last place in the world I would go to otherwise than bodily dragged (to the stake)" (5.22.65 HGL 27).

Again, in 1967, the Trappist expressed himself similarly with regard to the Roman ecclesiastical bureaucracy to the Belgian Benedictine Dom Jean Leclercq:

> With Rome as it is, renewal will always be a slow struggle. The whole conception of authority all down the line is not favorable to a really spontaneous renewal, but we can be glad that things are as good as they are and not worse. The dead concepts will continue for a while to usurp the place belonging to life, but I do not think it will really matter much—except that some monasteries may finally be closed down. Perhaps that will be for the better.
>
> . . . let us all hope we can manage to be at the same time obedient and free. It is not easy. But God is faithful, and that is my only hope. (2.17.67 SC 329)

Merton was far more respectful of and tolerant of the popes than he was of their curial officials. In a 1964 letter to Gordon Zahn, the Trappist compared the popes of his lifetime and pointed to the fallacy of the papal system: "Actually, the great question is the Papacy itself in its post-Tridentine and post-medieval, indeed post-Constantinian shape." He described Pius XII, the first pope he came to know after his 1938 conversion: "Pius was the curial Pope, the saint of the office types, the one whom the conservative cardinals overheard conversing with Christ in vision, the one whose cause was all lined up until Hochhuth as devil's advocate had his say, and very pertinently this had to be said for the good of the Church, to preserve us from the monstrous canonization of the Holy Office and of all the Curia with Pius" (7.2.64 HGL 652).

A few weeks later Merton again commented on the difficulties experienced by Pius XII and what appeared to be his failure to act to save Jews from the Holocaust of World War II. He noted that even the fathers of the church had sometimes "ranted against the Jews." This issue of the Vatican's evading such a catastrophe in the 1940s made Merton question whether too much authority is vested in one person in the Roman Church, namely, the pope.

One is faced with the evident truth that this shocking evasion
has been accepted without murmur by the whole Church for
centuries and not even the ghastly attempt of Hitler has really
awakened the Church to the enormity of it. Someone lent me
the Hochhuth play, a terrible piece of work and quite stupid,
but there is nevertheless a certain truth in it. There is this official, public way the Church has of being in the world, this
embodiment of authority in one figure who answers everything
and settles everything and who is therefore *expected* to have an
answer for everything . . . We could have been more humble.
(Ray Livingston, 5.11.64 WF 247)

Humility is what Thomas Merton found in the successor to
Pius. As he wrote to Mark Van Doren at the time of the election
of the patriarch of Venice, Angelo Giuseppe Roncalli, to the
papacy on October 28, 1958:

I think the new Pope [John XXIII] is a wonder, a fine simple old
man, who would not let anybody kiss his foot, and whose first
thought was to go back to his native village and have a fine
fiesta with his brothers and cousins. (Though it turns out he
probably can't go.) Whose first public statement, or one of the
first, was that the Pope doesn't have to know everything and
be able to do everything, and that all he has to be is the Pope.
I have written at once to say that he is my favorite Pope.
(11.20.58 RJ 32)

This loveable pope's convening of Vatican II only deepened
Thomas Merton's respect and love for this old man whose
courage opened the doors of the church toward reform and
renewal. As he wrote to Sr. Therese Lentfoehr at the conclusion
of the first conciliar session:

The Council was tremendous, wasn't it? (Isn't it?) Really Pope
John has been a great gift from God to all of us. What a superb
Pope, and what a heart. The past few months have made me
realize the greatness of the Church as I had never realized it
before, not the stuffed shirt pompous greatness that some of

the Curia people evidently want it to be, but the charity and the real concern for all men, the *cura pastoralis*. (12.20.62 RJ 243)

In late September of 1962 as the opening of the council neared, Pope John was diagnosed with stomach cancer. This information was withheld from the public until late November, lest it distract from the important work of Vatican II. When the gravity of the pope's illness became known, the Trappist wrote to the Russian Orthodox scholar Sergius Bolshakoff that he was "deeply grieved and worried" about the pope's illness. Merton offered high praise for Pope John: "He has done a great and providential work at the Council and is a very great Pope, one whom I personally love and revere as a true Father, and indeed I may say there is no man on earth for whom I have a deeper veneration, not only because of his office but also be-cause of his personal qualities" (12.28.62 HGL 102).

During Holy Week, 1963, as John XXIII was growing weaker and approaching death, Merton wrote to E. I. Watkin of his esteem for the pope: "I do think Pope John has been entirely providential, a great and fine Pope, and so much better than the last one. He has shown that a little initiative at Rome can really work great changes . . . This may be something to reckon with, and I hope much good will come out of it . . ." (Holy Thursday, 1963 HGL 584).

After John XXIII died on June 3, 1963, the Trappist expressed to several correspondents both his sadness and his appreciation for the kind of man the pope had been. To philosopher Leslie Dewart: "Pope John was certainly a great and unexpected blessing" (6.28.63 WF 294). To social activist James Forest: "Yes, the loss of Pope John is great, but he did an astonishing work in four and a half years. The Holy Spirit really moved in him, and I hope this will be true at the conclave and in the next Pope, whoever he may be" (6.7.63 HGL 274). To his poet-friend Sr. Therese Lentfoehr: "Pope John will, I think, be impossible to equal. No one can replace such a man. As time goes by we will see how extraordinary he really was. I have no doubt he was one of the great saints of our time" (6.30.63 RJ 245). And to Nicaraguan writer Pablo Antonio Cuadra: "Pope John [XXIII] was a profoundly human and genuine person, as well as a saint (I think the two must go together, for sanctity is destroyed by inhumanity no matter where it comes from and with no matter what good intentions)" (8.1.63 CT 190).

A few years later, after Merton had read *Journal of a Soul*, John XXIII's spiritual diary, he acknowledged that he was surprised to discover the simplicity and ordinariness of the pope's very traditional piety. It did not seem like the interior life of a person who would generate such an energy of reform in the church. In a letter to David Scott, who had sent Merton the proofs of this papal journal, the monk wrote:

> It was a great pleasure to receive Pope John's *Spiritual Journal* in proof. I had heard of the book and was very anxious to read it. It did not deceive my expectations. It is a record of deep piety and unquestionable sanctity, full of delightful and unexpected details about the inner life of a great and holy and utterly simple man. But I think the importance of the book lies partly in the fact that it is the expression of a very traditional and in some ways almost hackneyed spirituality. It is utterly *ordinary* in its content: there is nothing in the piety of Pope John that would surprise or disconcert the ordinary and average "faithful." This might at first sight seem strange to those who particularly appreciate the breath of renewal and change which began to sweep the Church when Angelo Roncalli became Pope John XXIII. But in fact it shows, to the Catholic mind, that the Johannine renewal was not a revolutionary break with the past but a charismatic fulfillment of the living and timeless demands of the Gospel. (1.25.65 WF 171–72)

In 1965 Merton sensed that John XXIII and he had had a good deal in common in their openness to the Word and in their efforts to break through to new paths.

> . . . I can say as a Christian, and an existentialist Christian, that I have often experienced the fact that the "moment of truth" in the Christian context is the encounter with the inscrutable word of God, the personal and living interpretation of the word of

God when it is lived, when it breaks through by surprise into our own completely contemporary and personal existence. And this means of course that it breaks through conventional religious routines and even seems in some ways quite scandalous in terms of the average and accepted interpretation of what religious ought to be. Hence, those for whom religion constitutes in effect a protection against any real moments of truth are people I cannot understand. I am glad that in our time we have had someone like Pope John, whose life amply demonstrates the validity, I think, of my view of it. (Mr. Wainwright, 7.10.65 WF 254)

Thomas Merton's thoughts about Pope John's successor, Giovanni Battista Montini, changed over the years. Shortly after the cardinal archbishop of Milan was elected to the see of Peter on June 21, 1963, the monk wrote in a positive vein about the new pope: "Pope John will, I think, be impossible to equal. No one can replace such a man. . . . Pope Paul will, however, be good in a different way. Bright, energetic, experienced, and I think holy also. Maritain thought very highly of him years ago when he was in the Secretariat, and whatever slight contacts I have had with him have always impressed me favorably" (Sr. Therese Lentfoehr, 6.30.63 RJ 245).

Merton's enthusiasm for the new pope continued into the fall of 1963. He had read Morris West's new novel, *The Shoes of the Fisherman*, while in the hospital and "thought it rather naïve & after all timid & passive." He judged that Pope Paul VI was "really much more energetic than the tense Pope of that novel! The recent pronouncements have been fine. Did I tell you he wrote me a personal letter & sent me an autographed picture? I expect great things from Pope Paul & this session of the Council . . ." (Lentfoehr, 10.3.63 RJ 246–47).

Following the second session of Vatican II, Merton began to have questions about the direction being taken by the new pope, especially in regard to the treatment of the Jews in the conciliar discussion. Papal political compromise was replacing courage and vision, as Merton saw it. "Now Paul's curial side has won over his Johannine heritage and the Jews are being forgotten for precisely the same reason, . . . in Moslem territory where, no matter what happens, the Church is going to have a rough time and fight a perhaps losing battle . . ." (Gordon Zahn, 7.2.64 HGL 653). At the close of the third session in December 1964, his doubts about the pope continued: ". . . The end of the Council session was not exactly encouraging. I know it was shattering for Fr. [Bernard] Haring, who wrote about it. He said it was shattering for Pope Paul also. I hear by all accounts that the Pope looks exhausted. His peace proposal at Bombay was impressive, however . . ." (Lentfoehr, 12.13.64 RJ 250). He was actually quite severe in his judgments of the pope in writing to Nicaraguan priest-poet Ernesto Cardenal that month:

> The ending of the Council session was very ambiguous and as a result the Protestants in this country have become once again quite dubious about the Church. They see that many bishops want more openness and liberty but they feel that the Pope [Paul VI] is on the side of an entrenched minority and I wonder if this is not perhaps quite true. The Pope does some very encouraging things, but one finds that he later tends to cancel them out and neutralize them by other acts or statements that are very conservative. Hence I suppose that we must be patient with a period of transition in which everything will still tend to be quite equivocal. The Church badly needs the prayers of all of us . . ." (12.24.64 CT 148)

By the fall of 1965, Thomas Merton was somewhat more impressed with the leadership of Pope Paul. This was because the pope seemed to be in harmony with the monk's judgments about the evils of war. In his strong speech to the United Nations Paul called for "No more war." Merton reacted:

> Whatever you have to say about peace, Pope Paul's speech at the U.N. certainly cleared things up a bit. I would say in parentheses that you should probably be a little critical of the term

pacifist, which implies a religious or ethical code based on the idea or article of faith that all war is by essence evil always and everywhere. The present position of most Catholics is that war has ceased to be a reasonable and just method of solving conflicts (I mean most modern Catholics who see that it is evil at all). . . . The position of the Pope and of the Council (I hope—I haven't seen what has been said) is that war can no longer be tolerated as the normal form of last resort in international conflicts, and this by reason of universally accepted moral norms. Much stronger . . . (Harry Cargas, 10.13.65 WF 170)

Such thoughts continued into early 1966: "There are hopes now that the Vietnam war may reach the conference table, thanks largely to the efforts of Paul VI. Something to be very thankful for" (Jean and Hildegard Goss-Mayr, 1.14.66 HGL 337).

Twice during 1967 Merton spoke of Paul VI in his correspondence. While still speaking of his devotion to his saintly predecessor, the monk acknowledged a filial relationship to the present pope in a letter to a young Italian correspondent who had recently visited Pope John's birthplace:

Thank you for your prayers which you have said you would offer me at Sotto il Monte, the village of our dear Pope John. He was very good to me and I felt that he was personally a Father as he took the trouble to send me good words and do me a kindness that I greatly appreciated. I have a very special love and veneration for Pope John whom I believe to be one of the great saints of the Church. Naturally I also have a filial devotion to our present Holy Father. (Mario Falsina, 3.25.67 RJ 350)

And, in a jocose mood, the monk wrote to a lawyer friend, John Slate, of the end of legalism that would come to the church under the Montini papacy: "I have partly recovered from social life due to Dan [Walsh]'s ordination and am once again in a state of unruffled stoicism. Meanwhile, though you are indeed busy, you are perhaps unaware that this is a purely temporary condition as all law is about to be abolished by Johnny Montini and you will find yourself with plenty of time to visit here with your wife. Be prepared . . ." (5.30.67 RJ 302). The lawyer escaped all law by a sudden and untimely death on September 19, 1967. In a sympathy note to his widow, Mary Ellen Slate, the monk reflected on the time of life he and his contemporaries were entering. His Columbia friend, artist Ad Reinhardt, had died suddenly not long before. "And with Ad Reinhardt's death just a week or two ago, I had been thinking how all of us are pretty much on the toboggan slide" (9.22.67 RJ 301).

5

On Ecumenism

Thomas Merton engaged in ecumenical dialogue with Jewish, Orthodox, and Protestant contacts during the late 1950s and early 1960s. He wrote of this to his poet-friend Sr. Therese Lentfoehr in May 1961: "Mostly I am busy with class and with Protestants . . ." (5.10.61 RJ 238). And again several months later one senses the broad base of the monk's ecumenical contacts and his sense of the societal difficulties involved in such work:

> . . . I am now seeing quite a lot of the various retreatants, particularly Protestants still. Also a wonderful Rabbi from Winnipeg a Hasid [Zalman Schachter]: an orthodox priest, a Negro working on fair labor practices for Negroes, and lots of others like that. They are wonderful people, and have so much. It is very encouraging, except that there does not seem to be much they can do with all the good that is in them, in the face of the evil that threatens everyone. I can still get mad at society, all right. It is such a tragic thing that society as a whole should be so violent, corrupt, wasteful, and absurd . . . (9.19.61 RJ 238–39)

He wrote at the same time of these endeavors to Nicaraguan writer Pablo Antonio Cuadra: "I have been busy with many

80

interesting meetings and conferences with Protestant theologians, writers and others" (9.16.61 CT 189–90).

While Thomas Merton appreciated these exchanges with Protestants, he was aware of the limitations of such dialogue for institutional reform and reunion. "One thing here is that I am having occasional meetings with good and earnest Protestant seminary professors, and we sit and talk and discover how much we really agree on many things and that if we cannot change the situation about our respective groups, we perhaps are not expected to change it. But that there are many other things we can change in ourselves. This I think can be fruitful" (John Harris, 6.17.60 HGL 396).

Merton's approach to Christian unity and to the unity among all religions was not grounded primarily in discussing differences in creed, code, and cult. Merton's was a much more personal, spiritual, and experiential approach. He wrote about this to John Harris in 1959. In Merton's view salvation is a gift from God that is not primarily reliant on one's relationship with any religious institution or structure or doctrine.

> For Christ speaks in us only when we speak as men to one another and not as members of something, officials, or what have you. Though of course there are official declarations and official answers: but they never come anywhere near the kind of thing you bring up, which is personal. No one is officially saved, salvation *cannot* be that kind of thing. The other reason for not claiming to answer all your questions and solve all your problems is that I really don't think your problems are as real as they seem to be: they are indeed, or they tend to be, created by the whole false position arising out of the fact that there are so many who insist on having, and giving, official solutions. As I say, declarations can and must be made but they never get into the depths where a person finds himself in God. You may think me flippant if I say you probably believe in God already, and your problem consists not in whether or not you doubt God, but in trying to account to yourself for a belief in God which does not sound like anything official you have ever heard

about this matter. And in wondering whether, that being the case, it is "the same God" you believe in.

Whatever may be the intellectual aspects of the thing—I leave them to you, only suggesting that you do not have to apply yourself madly to "working" anything "out." If at the same time you can read and enjoy books by me and by Pasternak it is clear that you are a basically religious person. And in that case, explanations and manipulations of symbols are not the most important thing but the reality of your life in God. The symbols can later take care of themselves . . . (1.31.59 HGL 385–86)

During 1961 Thomas Merton was engaged extensively in Protestant-Catholic dialogue. A cinder block cottage had been erected in the woods near the abbey to house these conversations. This was the place that would become Merton's hermitage in 1965. He wrote about these ecumenical encounters to Nicaraguan priest-poet Ernesto Cardenal:

There is no telling what is to become of the work I have attempted with the Protestant ministers and scholars. Evidently someone has complained to Rome about my doing work that is "not fitting for a contemplative" and there have been notes of disapproval. The contacts will have to be cut down to a minimum. I do not mind very much, personally. I have the hermitage and would rather use it as a hermitage than as a place for retreat conferences. In all this I remain pretty indifferent, as a matter of fact. There are much wider perspectives to be considered. My concept of the Church, my faith in the Church, has been and is being tested and purified: I hope it is being purified. Even my idea of "working for the Church" is being radically changed. I have less and less incentive to take any kind of initiative in promising anything for the immediate visible apostolic purposes of the Church. It is not easy for me to explain what I feel about the movements that proliferate everywhere, and the generosity and zeal that goes into them all. But in the depths of my heart I feel very empty about all that, and there is in me a growing sense that it is all provisional and perhaps has very little of the meaning that these zealous promoters attribute to it. So about any contacts I may have had with Protestants. I have had just enough to know how ambiguous it all becomes. The only result has been to leave me with a profound respect and love for these men, and an increased understanding of their spirit. But at the same time I am not sanguine about the chances of a definite "movement" for reunion, and, as I say, I am left with the feeling that the "movement" is not the important thing. As if there were something more hidden and more important, which is also much easier to attain, and is yet beyond the reach of institutional pressures. (12.24.61 CT 129)

By May of 1962, although Merton was enjoying time in his "hermitage" more and more, he was wearying of these ecumenical dialogues, as he wrote to Cardenal:

. . . The frequent retreats of Protestants and others keep me unusually busy. The hermitage is fine. I take advantage of it as much as possible. This life takes on a new dimension when one actually has time to begin to meditate! Otherwise it is not really serious, just a series of exercises which one offers up with a pure intention and with the hope that they mean something. That is not what the monastic life is for. (5.16.62 CT 132)

Abraham Heschel, the Jewish rabbi and theologian from New York, was one of Merton's principal correspondents regarding Christian and Jewish relations. In 1960 the Trappist wrote to Heschel: "I believe humbly that Christians and Jews ought to realize together something of the same urgency of expectation and desire, even though there is a radically different theological dimension to their hopes. They remain the same hopes with altered perspectives. It does not seem to me that this is ever emphasized" (12.17.60 HGL 431).

In 1963 Merton discussed with Heschel some of the issues between Jews and Christians regarding the prophets of the Hebrew Scriptures:

Merton judged that he and the Shakers had much in common spiritually despite their theological divergences, as he wrote to Andrews:

> I have allowed myself to be involved in more tasks and interests than I should, and the one that has most suffered has been the study of the Shakers. It is in a way so completely out of the theological realm with which I am familiar, although their spirit has so much in common with ours. . . .
>
> It is very certain that the Shakers preserved many many deeply important religious symbols and lived out some of the most basic religious myths in their Christian and gnostic setting. I cannot help feeling also that the very existence of the Shakers at that particular moment of history has a very special significance, a sort of "prophetic" function in relation to what has come since. (8.22.61 HGL 35)

One of Merton's lifelong quests was the search for truth. And in this he found another commonality with the Shakers: "The Shakers remain as witnesses to the fact that only humility keeps man in communion with truth, and first of all with his own inner truth. This one must know without knowing it, as they did. For as soon as a man becomes aware of 'his truth' he lets go of it and embraces an illusion" (Andrews, 12.21.61 HGL 36).

In the fall of 1962 Merton wrote to Andrews of some Shaker problems that had arisen at Shirley Meeting House. They reflected some of his own concerns with the vocation to monastic life, since in both situations, ". . . the law of all spiritual life is the law of risk and struggle, and possible failure." Merton continued:

> Perhaps somewhere in the mystery of Shaker "absolutism" which in many ways appears to be "intolerant" and even arbitrary, there is an underlying gentleness and tolerance and understanding that appears not in words but in life and in work. It is certainly in the songs. Some of us only learn tolerance and understanding after having been intolerant and "absolute."

In a word, it is hard to live with a strict and sometimes almost absurd ideal, and the ambivalence involved can be tragic, or salutary. More than anything else, the Shakers faced that risk and the fruitfulness of their life was a sign of approval upon their daring. (9.20.62 HGL 37)

A few months later Merton noted that for Shakers, as well as for monks, the foundation on which their lives are based is an obedience in faith: "And of course it is for us in our own way by our faith and obedience to all of God's 'words' to attune ourselves to His will and to join in His work, according to our own humble capacities. The Shakers saw this so well, and saw that their work was a cooperation in the same will that framed and governs the cosmos: and more governs history" (Andrews, 12.28.62 HGL 37–38).

Following Andrews's death in 1964, Merton wrote to his widow of his profound appreciation for the Shaker tradition. "I realize more and more the vital importance of the Shaker 'gift of simplicity' which is a true American charism . . ." (Mrs. Edward Deming Andrews, 7.20.64 HGL 40). As he had written to her husband in 1962: "The 'Gift to be Simple' is in fact the 'Gift to be True,' and what we need most in our life today, personal, national and international, is this truth. . . . There is more in this than just a pious song" (9.20.62 HGL 37).

Merton's own personal and spiritual approach to ecumenical activities led him toward the Holy Spirit who, he believed, would lead all religions in a common search for truth. He wrote of this in 1963 to Sergius Bolshakoff during the time of Spirit-inspired Vatican II. "I am very drawn to the Russian idea of *sobornost* [the doctrine of the Spirit acting and leading the whole church into the truth] which seems to me to be essential to the notion of the Church, in some form or other. I do not know how this can be gainsaid. Collegiality is a step in that direction" (11.11.63 HGL 104).

Perhaps some of Thomas Merton's most profound writings about ecumenism can be found in a series of letters with his English friend Etta Gullick between 1963 and 1966. His thoughts very much reflected the discussions at Vatican II about the mystery of the church. He also paraphrased, consciously or unconsciously, the words of John XXIII in his opening address at the council: "For the substance of the ancient deposit of faith is one thing, and the way in which it is presented is another" (Peter Hebblethwaite, *Pope John XXIII: Pope of the Century*, 223).

> We cannot get too deep into the mystery of our oneness in Christ. It is so deep as to be unthinkable and yet a little thought about it doesn't hurt. But it doesn't help too much either. The thing is that we are not united in a *thought* of Christ or a desire of Christ, but in His Spirit. . . . there is all the difference in the world between theology as *experienced* (which is basically identical in all who know and love Christ, at least in its root) and theology as *formulated* in which there can be great differences. In the former, it is the One Spirit who teaches and enlightens us. In the second it is the Church, and in this of course I believe that the Roman Church is the only one that can claim to say the last word. But I do not think it makes sense to be narrowly Roman in a sort of curial-party sense, and I am also very attracted to the orthodox *sobornost* idea. And of course I think in reality Pope John has been quietly moving in that direction, and he has been perfectly right in so doing, without affecting his own primacy and so on. . . . I do not of course intend a hard-and-fast distinction between the Spirit on one hand teaching the individual and the Church teaching him: this would be erroneous. But I mean the Spirit teaching us all interiorly, and also exteriorly through the magisterium. In either case it is the Spirit of the Church, and the Church, living and speaking. But in exterior doctrinal formulations, where there are different groups, there are various confusions and differences. And so on. I am not a very sharp technical theologian, as you can see. (Gullick, 4.29.63 HGL 359–60)

In 1965 the Trappist, again reflecting the discussions at Vatican II, wrote to Gullick of the role of the Holy Spirit in leading the church toward deeper unity: "It is the Holy Spirit who makes us one and our experience of Him may or may not make much difference. But faith in Him makes a very great deal of difference and this is the important thing. Deep faith and obedience. I see this more and more. So let us be united in prayer in Christ and in His Spirit" (6.9.65 HGL 371).

After the conclusion of Vatican II, it was clear to Merton that the institutional reunion of the Christian churches was not yet possible. Still he believed that, in the Spirit, a real unity already existed among Christian people and their churches. From his contemplative vantage point the monk wrote again to Gullick:

> . . . there can be little hope of institutional or sacramental union as yet between Anglicans and Romans. Perhaps on the other hand I am too stoical about it all, but I frankly am not terribly anguished. I am not able to get too involved in the institutional side of any of the efforts now being made as I think, for very many reasons, they are bound to be illusory in large measure. And this kind of thing is for others who know more about it. To me it is enough to be united with people in love and in the Holy Spirit, as I am sure I am, and they are, in spite of the sometimes momentous institutional and doctrinal differences. But where there is a sincere desire for truth and real good will and genuine love, there God Himself will take care of the differences far better than any human or political ingenuity can. Prayer is the thing, and union with the suffering Lord on His Cross . . . (11.24.66 HGL 378)

One can note at this point the Trappist's earlier expression of qualified admiration of Anglicanism in a letter to Oxford scholar A. M. Allchin in 1964: "It seems to me that the best of Anglicanism is unexcelled, but that there are few who have the refinement of spirit to see and embrace the best, and so many who fall off into the dreariest rationalism" (4.25.64 HGL 26).

During the mid-1960s Thomas Merton's external ecumenical interests and activities were turned more in the direction of shared action among religionists for human and societal concerns. He wrote about this to Gordon Zahn in 1963:

> . . . the climate of ecumenism is all very nice, but does it have all the wonderful meaning we read into it? Christ said: If you salute your brethren, what are you doing that the pagans have not done? I don't think that the glad gatherings of people who are exactly alike in every respect except their commitment to slightly different religious forms are exactly a presage of world peace. If they gathered together for something significant, like peace and disarmament, or the race issue, it would make more sense and I might find encouragement in it. (4.30.63 HGL 650)

By 1964, while Merton was still meeting with Protestants at the cottage in the woods as well as in the monastery, he wrote to Cardenal: "There have been meetings of Protestants here often, but I do not want to overdo this" (5.8.64 CT 145). In the following spring, as Merton prepared to move into the cottage as his hermitage, he wrote to Sr. Therese Lentfoehr of his shift of emphasis away from ecumenical involvements:

> There is a blessing on every attempt at ecumenism that is simple and sincere, and your desire to do this not for your own sake but for God and the Church and for them, will guarantee that it will be blessed in one way or another. I am not in any ecumenical work this year. Fr. Abbot wanted me to withdraw from it as I am planning more and more to be in the hermitage and perhaps even live there eventually. I must meet his requirements therefore, and am not sorry to. (3.27.65 RJ 250)

In June 1966, Merton the hermit wrote about the decline in his ecumenical engagements to his aunt Agnes Merton living in New Zealand. He also expressed himself to be not totally "Roman" in his Catholicism.

> I am not working with ecumenical groups at the moment. Since I came up to the hermitage Fr. Abbot feels I ought not to do any kind of active work with people, and I am not terribly anxious to unless it should turn out to be necessary . . . . I have lots of Anglican contacts . . . . All High Churchy as you might well imagine. But I am a pretty liberal bloke myself, if not radical.

Actually I feel very much at home with the C. of E. except when
people are awfully stuffy and insular about it. I have never been
and will never be aggressively Roman, by any means. It would
not be possible for a Merton to go too far with a really "popish"
outlook. We are all too hardheaded and independent. (6.1.66
RJ 75)

By 1967 Merton's interests had clearly grown from ecumenism toward interreligious dialogue. After years of noncom-
munication with his uncle and aunt, Harold and Elsie Jenkins,
who were his mother's brother and his wife, Merton wrote to
them of his growing interest in Buddhism: ". . . I see a lot of
ministers and others on an 'ecumenical' basis. My main interest
in that line however is keeping up with Buddhists, especially
Zen people. They are the ones for whom I seem to have the
closest affinities. We get along quite well . . ." (12.31.67 RJ 83).

Thomas Merton's final comments about ecumenism in his
published letters are expressed in an April 1968 letter to a high
school junior at St. Thomas Seminary in Bloomfield, Connecti-
cut, named Philip J. Cascia. The young man had written to
Merton about his term paper on ecumenism and Merton's
general response was generally affirming of the ecumenical
movement: "I'd say that the ecumenical movement is certainly
an excellent thing, and it has meant new life for all Christians.
Of course it is something of a fad in some places, and it gets
the usual distorted kind of publicity. But basically it is a good
thing" (4.10.68 RJ 36).

6

On Priesthood

Thomas Merton's awareness of his call to the priesthood came not long after his baptism as a Roman Catholic at Corpus Christi Church in New York City, in 1938. His mentor, Dan Walsh, called this potential vocation to Merton's attention in 1939. He said, "You know, the first time I met you I thought you had a vocation to the priesthood" (*Reader*, 95).

Merton made a kind of pilgrimage to Cuba in the spring of 1940, and was very moved spiritually at the Basilica of Our Lady of Cobre. It was there that he prayed to become a priest. He invoked Our Lady: ". . . you will ask Christ to make me His priest, and I will give you my heart, Lady" (*Reader*, 79).

Merton first pursued his vocation to the priesthood through the Franciscan Order. But when he revealed to one of their priests that he impregnated a woman while a student at Cambridge University, that friar discouraged Merton from pursuing a Franciscan vocation. Merton was crushed and felt this to be a sign that he did not have a vocation to priesthood (Michael Mott, *The Seven Mountains of Thomas Merton*, 156).

In the summer of 1941, after sensing that his vocation to priesthood had been blocked, Tom Merton talked with Catherine de Hueck Doherty about possibly coming to work with her among the poor in Harlem. Of that desire he wrote:

. . . the first thing to do is to feed the poor and save the souls
of men, and in this sense, feeding the poor means feeding them
not by law (which doesn't do a damn bit of good), but first of
all at the cost of our own appetites, and with our own hands,
and for the love of God. In that case, feeding the poor and saving them are all part of the same thing, the love of our neighbor
. . . (10.6.41 HGL 5)

After writing so many words in this letter Merton declared
one thing about his calling which would prove prophetic: ". . .
my vocation is probably to go on finding out this same thing
about writing over and over as long as I live: when you are
writing about God, or talking about Him, you are doing something you were created to do, even if you don't feel like a prince
every minute you are doing it . . ." (10.6.41 HGL 6).

Doherty suggested to Merton that anyone asking the kinds
of questions he was asking "probably wanted to be a priest."
He was surprised and scared when she said this. "The priest
business is something I am supposed to be all through and
done with. I nearly entered the Franciscans. There was a very
good reason why I didn't, and now I am convinced that Order
is not for me and never was. So that settles that vocation"
(11.10.41 HGL 7).

In the previous year Tom had told his Columbia mentor,
Mark Van Doren, of his high views of the priestly life: "To be
a priest does not mean that you are necessarily perfect but that
you are solemnly bound to a manner of life in which you observe all those things pertaining to perfection" (6.16.40 RJ 8).
Merton was teaching at St. Bonaventure College, a Franciscan
school in Olean, New York, at the time. For him it was "a sort
of harmless hobby: about on the plane of stamp collecting. In
any visible results it may have, as regards the Kingdom of God,
it is just about as valuable as stamp collecting, too." Merton
told Doherty that he realized this teaching was "strictly temporary . . . I don't know what it is that will help me to serve
God better: but whatever it is, it doesn't seem to be here. Something is missing" (11.10.41 HGL 7).

During Holy Week, 1941, at the suggestion of Dan Walsh, Merton made a retreat at the Cistercian Abbey of Gethsemani near Bardstown in Kentucky. There he sensed a strong attraction to the strict and silent Trappist way of life. Later that year Merton left St. Bonaventure College on December 8, 1941, the day after the Japanese attack on Pearl Harbor, in order to join the Trappists in Kentucky. He wrote to Doherty that he was finally following his call: "You see, I have always wanted to be a priest . . ." Merton explained that he now knew that he was not called to serve the poor in Harlem.

The draft board was going to reclassify him for military service, and he asked to be deferred to pursue a monastic vocation. Of this he wrote to Doherty:

> I don't desire *anything* in the world, not writing, not teaching, not any kind of consolation or outward activity: I simply long with my whole existence to be completely consecrated to God in every gesture, every breath and every movement of my body and mind, to the exclusion of absolutely everything except Him: and the way I desire this, by His grace, is the way it is among the Trappists. . . . I am unshakably rooted in faith in this vocation: but there is the army [that] may try to kill it in me. (12.6.41 HGL 9–11)

After theological studies in his monastic community, Merton was ordained to the priesthood at Gethsemani Abbey by Louisville's Archbishop John A. Floersch on May 26, 1949, and given the name "Louis." As ordination neared the monk expressed his quite exalted and elated thoughts and feelings about the upcoming event to Mark Van Doren. Merton's view at that time of the greater importance of ordination over religious vows would surely change over the coming years.

> I know the priesthood is going to be something tremendous. A kind of death, to begin with. But that is good. The whole business about Orders has been striking me as something much more important than religious vows. The question of sacramen-

tal character comes in, for one thing. Then you become public property. At the same time you are mystically more isolated in God. The combination is quite baffling.

Anyway, the priesthood will end up by giving me a completely social function. Perhaps that was what I was always trying to escape. Actually, having run into it at this end of the circle, it is making me what I was always meant to be and I am about to exist.

As soon as I put on the vestments of a subdeacon and stood in the sanctuary I was bowled over by the awareness that this was what I was always supposed to wear, and everything else, so far, had been something of a disguise. (4.8.49 RJ 23)

On the day of Fr. Louis's ordination, Robert Lax, Merton's close friend from Columbia University, commented that Merton looked much younger than his age. He was playful and joyful after the ceremony (William H. Shannon, *Silent Lamp: The Thomas Merton Story*, 140). Merton himself sensed that he had finally fulfilled the promise he made at the Church of Our Lady of Cobre in 1940 (Mott, *Seven Mountains*, 251).

During the 1960s, Merton moved beyond some of his earlier and more pious views of the priesthood. He became more realistic about what it is and what it is not to serve as priest. As he wrote to Daniel Berrigan in 1962: "I find I have reached the stage where I involuntarily wince when I come upon another poem by a priest called 'Vocation'" (3.10.62 HGL 73). Again, in a 1964 letter to the Jesuit poet, the Trappist seemed to find many of the postconciliar concerns about priestly reform of diminishing concern and interest to him. "What is the Society doing about *aggiornamento*? Do you have a vocation problem? Are you doing something new about religious formation? I don't know, perhaps those questions do not really matter as much as they seem to. I am not totally convinced of the importance that is attributed to them" (9.19.64 HGL 85).

By 1962, Thomas Merton, the monk and the priest, had grown into a quite different sense of his priestly and monastic vocation when he wrote to Abdul Aziz:

completely with a Church (like the ordinary priest) or a party (like the Communists). (1.17.66 CT 228)

That same year, 1966, in light of Vatican II and the postconciliar period of reform, Thomas Merton was clearly feeling himself some of the great strains that priests had in their relationships with bishops and superiors. Priests seemed to be experiencing both a deep crisis of identity and a painful crisis of authority. One such priest, William DuBay of the Archdiocese of Los Angeles, became the focus of the monk's correspondence about the troubles in the priesthood.

W. H. Ferry had discussed the challenge DuBay made to his archbishop, James Cardinal McIntyre, and mentioned to Merton DuBay's proposal to establish a priests' union. In his response the monk showed his awareness of the limitations of superiors in their relations with priests, and he saw these relationships as part of the reason for clerical immaturity. To Merton, the proposal for a priests' union seemed to be a symptom of such immaturity.

> . . . [E]ven in the Council it was spelled out that the relations with ecclesiastical Superiors were not what they should be, and it was also said, in traditional terms, that the Superiors ought to get down to the business of mending their ways. The trouble is of course that they can't. They don't see the problems the way subjects do, especially if they have been in a Chancery Office for years, twenty, thirty, forty, some of them. And think of those characters who have been in the Vatican since they were teenagers practically. They just have no idea what the score is, and they don't know how to look squarely at the problems of subjects, especially they do not and cannot understand the difference between the real problems of creative initiative and the neurotic kid problems that, in fact, they generate in subjects and unconsciously like to perpetuate. The relations of Superiors and subjects, in religion and in the secular clergy, are very often completely puerile, centered on artificial and illusory problems which are almost deliberately kept going because they create an illusion of important decisions being made. All this nonsense could be avoided with a minimum of maturity.

. . . the Superiors are never going to solve it themselves. On the other hand, the Superiors respond only to pressure. And we cannot get higher Superiors to bring pressure on lower Superiors, they are all in cahoots like a gang of thieves, and all support one another in tricky procedures, secret power plays, cheating, etc. etc. Hence the only thing to do is to bring pressure from the secular arm so to speak. . . .

In my opinion, I think that the risks of this approach should be studied objectively. . . . Personally, I think that it will do a great deal of harm to the Church, if it is not handled with extreme tact and care . . . But I think nevertheless, theologically and biblically, we have to ascertain whether the Church is the kind of body that can stand such a thing as a priest's union without getting into schism. I think that the fact that they start out uncritically making no distinction between a labor union and a "priest's union" shows that there is danger of being wrong from the beginning, because, however you look at it, the relation of a priest to his bishop is not that of an employee to an employer. Hence the problems that arise between them, and the very real question of the priest's rights, need to be expressed in a different form. . . .

My frank opinion on this is that instead of forming a priests' union and causing public pressure with a lot of noise in the press, priests should form a kind of private association for settling their problems in the more or less "regular" way, and it would be understood that instead of appealing to outside pressure they would make it understood that if they continued to get the runaround they would simply get out, get secularized, and use their talents in some other way where they would be less obstructed. The need of priests is considerable these days, but is presented in artificial statistical sort of language which is really bypassing all issues. Yet it scares the bishops. If they realize that they are just not going to have any decent priests left, and that they will be stuck with aged cranks, creeps, seventy-year-old infants and so on . . . they may think things over. (Ferry, 1.26.66 HGL 223–25)

The Trappist's proposal of a "private association" for priests to deal with superiors was a more reasonable approach than the concept of a priests' union. In places like the Archdiocese of Chicago such a tactic was taken with success in the formation of the Association of Chicago Priests as they dealt with the authoritarian style of John Cardinal Cody during the 1970s. Two months later, in 1966, Thomas Merton wrote to Ferry with further expressions of opposition to DuBay's unionizing approach to ecclesiastical superiors:

> . . . the kind of collision course with authority that he advocates is not going to get anywhere really. The whole situation is already so vitiated with politics that his ideas will only make it ultra-political. The whole source of the authority problem in the Church is precisely that Superiors act too much as politicians and manipulate subjects for purely institutional ends. Du Bay's course seems to point to an even worse kind of institutionalism in the long run. (3.11.66 HGL 225)

During 1968, the final year of life for Thomas Merton, he was offering what some in officialdom might have considered subversive advice to an anonymous priest who could not decide whether to stay or leave the active ministry. To "Father D.," the monk wrote something of the way he himself had come to understand and to live his own monastic and priestly vocation from his hermitage in the woods:

> Couldn't you be a sort of "underground priest" in lay clothes, saying Mass in private homes among people you are at ease with, and perhaps also serving some tiny community, some convent, and helping out with shut-ins, people who are forgotten, who suffer, etc.? In other words it seems to me that in this Post-Conciliar period you might be called to a kind of hidden service in the sort of unofficial and informal life you desire. In short, be like a layman, live like a layman, but do some priestly work or service along with it.
>
> I don't see that you have to stop being a priest just because the routine machinery of parish organization is bugging you. All the more reason to get out of the ordinary patterns and yet to be a priest nevertheless, and work in a quiet, relaxed relationship with people you can relate to without too much difficulty.

After all, you are always going to have to relate to people. See your priesthood not as a role or an office, but as just part of your own life and your own relation to other persons. You can bring them Christ in some quiet way, and perhaps you will find yourself reaching people that the Church would not otherwise contact. (3.14.68 SC 371)

The final words of Thomas Merton about priesthood that are found in his published letters are these short and cryptic remarks made in his characteristic and usual "unusual" style of correspondence with Robert Lax during the month of June, shortly before his death: "Brothers is all agog over the tempo. Was here a phalanx of novice masters a big drag an odious passatempo was come to the hermit box for a speech. 'You might as well all leave the clericals' I suggested with a wry leer. Was cheered wildly for this" (6.22.68 RJ 185).

At the time of his early and sudden death in Bangkok, Thailand, on December 10, 1968, Thomas Merton had surely shifted considerably in his sense of and reflections on the Roman Catholic priesthood, since the exalted experience of his ordination in May of 1949. And so had many of his brother priests around the world!

7

On Being a Hermit

Thomas Merton had always sought solitude and silence in his life. As he wrote in *The Seven Storey Mountain*:

> What I needed was the solitude to expand in breadth and depth and to be simplified out under the gaze of God more or less the way a plant spreads out its leaves in the sun. That meant that I needed a Rule that was almost entirely aimed at detaching me from the world and uniting me with God, not a Rule made to fit me to fight for God in the world. But I did not find out all that in one day. (*Reader*, 96)

As he was deciding, in the fall of 1941, whether to work with Catherine de Hueck Doherty at Friendship House in the slums of Harlem, or to enter the Abbey of Gethsemani, Tom Merton sought the Lord's will by opening the Bible as Augustine had once done in order to discern the divine mind. Whatever page he found, he thought, would perhaps help him to know his calling in life. He opened to the passage in the Gospel of Luke in which Zechariah was struck dumb by the angel. The words were: "you will be silent." He took this as a sign that he was meant to join "the burnt men" at the abbey of silence in the Kentucky hills. As he was to write in 1961: ". . . our life as monks is lived especially under the sign of a kind of inner solitude and dereliction, and I know from experience that this is true. But in this solitude and dereliction we are united with others who are alone and solitary and poor" (Abdul Aziz, 1.30.61 HGL 47).

Father Merton's formative years in the monastery deepened his desire—indeed, his deep need—for more solitude and silence. At times he thought of becoming a Camaldolese hermit in California or of joining a Carthusian charterhouse for greater solitude away from busy community life. His superiors always discouraged, and indeed, forbade such a move. Gradually, though, Merton was given permission by his abbot, Dom James Fox, to spend more and more time alone in the woods. In the spring of 1961 the Trappist wrote to his Chinese scholar friend John Wu about his delight in spending time alone in nature. "Now I enjoy the quiet of the woods and the song of birds and the presence of the Lord in silence. Here is Nameless Tao, revealed as Jesus, the brightness of the hidden Father, our joy and our life . . ." (5.19.61 HGL 617).

In April of 1960 Thomas Merton wrote about his desires for eremitical living to the French theologian Jean Danielou, SJ. He wrote of what he called his "vocation problem" at that time, which revolved around his need for greater solitude and silence.

> . . . I have consulted the psychiatrist in Louisville, who tells me that I am not neurotic and that my problem here in the monastery is quite a natural reaction to the situation. He feels, as you did last year, that it would help me to get away from the monastery now and again and renew my perspective. He also suggested the possibility of my withdrawing to the mountains of Kentucky to found a small annex to my own monastery for the purposes I had originally, remarking that since the "glory" of this would redound on the monastery there might be less objection to it. I have not given the matter much thought because I don't think the proposal would be well received, and at any rate I am not prepared to make it at this time as I have no plan, and do not feel like making one. (4.21.60 HGL 135)

The remarks about "glory" in the eremitical life probably refer to the charges leveled against him in 1958 by the psychoanalyst and recent Catholic convert Gregory Zilboorg, during a monastic meeting at St. John's Abbey in Collegeville, Minnesota. The doctor claimed to have "analyzed" Merton from his writings. Merton was told by the doctor at that time that his desire to become a hermit was a kind of neurotic, narcissistic grandstanding act on his part. Merton was deeply disturbed by these comments, both resenting and resisting their accuracy (Michael Mott, *The Seven Mountains of Thomas Merton*, 294–99).

Not long afterward Dom James permitted Fr. Louis to spend some time now and then in a small shed that Merton dubbed St. Anne's Hermitage. There he prayed and wrote and simply "lived." At one point during those years he proposed living as a hermit on top of the fire tower on Vintage Nob to the west of the abbey. A small cinder block conference center for ecumenical dialogues was constructed in 1960 on a hillside about one mile from the monastery, and Fr. Louis had designs on that spot from the beginning as his desired hermitage.

To Etta Gullick, the Trappist wrote in the fall of 1961 about his conviction that everyone needs a measure of quiet and aloneness to remain human.

> As for the call to solitude it is in some respects unavoidable, and imperative, and even if you are prevented by circumstances (e.g., marriage!) from doing anything about it, solitude will come and find you anyway, and this is not always the easiest thing in life either. It may take the form of estrangement, and really it shouldn't. But it does. However, that should not be sought or even too eagerly consented to. On the contrary. In any case the right result should be a great purity of heart and selflessness and detachment. (9.9.61 HGL 346)

In the spring of 1962 Merton expressed to Daniel Berrigan, SJ, how important the life of solitude and silence is for some within the church, as well as how the solitary's vocation is one lived out for the sake of the whole church.

There is an absolute need for the solitary, bare, dark, beyond-concept, beyond-thought, beyond-feeling type of prayer. Not of course for everybody. But unless that dimension is there in the Church somewhere, the whole caboodle lacks life and light and intelligence. It is a kind of hidden, secret, unknown stabilizer, and a compass too. About this I have no hesitations and no doubts, because it is my vocation . . . in it one feels the hand of God pressing down on him. (3.10.62 HGL 73)

Trappist life for many years had been strictly coenobitic. Monks were required to live a strict life of silence in community. But by late 1964 Fr. Louis had become convinced, through his monastic studies, that the eremitical life had also been part of the Cistercian tradition in its earlier years, and he conveyed that thought to Catherine de Hueck Doherty. He even mentioned the little cinder block house built as a conference center in the Gethsemani woods that would one day become his hermitage.

There is no question that the hermit life is a legitimate and traditional development of the monastic vocation. . . . in the monastic Orders we are going to frankly face the need of allowing temporary or permanent hermitages for some of our members. And in fact I already have a dacha or something, which I suppose is somewhat like yours, though perhaps bigger because it was originally built to house groups of ministers coming for dialogue. (11.21.64 HGL 21)

Two years earlier the monk had written to Doherty approving her Poustinia project. These were small hermitages at her retreat center in Canada that created much needed spaces for strictly silent retreats.

It is the kind of thing that is most needed. And though it is certain that we must speak if and when we can, silence is always more important. The crises of the age are so enormous and the mystery of evil so unfathomable: . . . all these things should show us that the real way is prayer, and penance, and closeness to God in poverty and solitude. Yet there is no question that sometimes this too is also preached as an invasion of responsibility. . . .

So it is usually when I have just resolved firmly to be perfectly silent that I find I have to speak: and when I have resolved to speak out boldly, that I am reduced to silence. (11.12.62 HGL 19–20)

By the spring and early summer of 1964 Merton was spending some daytime hours at the cinder block cottage in the woods but, as he wrote to his Pakistani Sufi correspondent, Abdul Aziz, he desired more of this treasured solitude and silence. "Actually the best I can do is spend the day in the hermitage, having to return to the monastery at night to sleep as it is strictly forbidden to sleep outside the enclosure walls . . ." (6.28.64 HGL 59). He expressed himself similarly to Daniel Berrigan: "I have decided that I have to have a very clear position on solitude . . . non-traveling and staying put in the woods have come to be essential to my whole life and vocation. This also means keeping contacts with the outside on a certain informal plane and always non-organized and offbeat" (5.18.64 HGL 81–82).

By November of that year Merton was quite frustrated that the monastic system was so slow in allowing him to move into the hermitage. He wrote of this to Catherine de Hueck Doherty:

As for the "hermit," well, the danger is that there is no precedent among us and no one to lead the way. . . .

I am involved in this myself, and have definite hopes of living in a hermitage here in the woods sometime in the not too distant future. . . . unfortunately people have a mania for organization and complication, trying to draw up detailed programs for everything all the time, and they forget to just live. (11.21.64 HGL 22)

The following month, however, Merton was relieved to be told that he could now sleep overnight in the hermitage sometimes without the constant interruption involved in following the monastic schedule of canonical hours. As he wrote to Aziz, "I am now able to sleep in the hermitage and may perhaps be able to arrange something like a decent retreat, if I can get a whole day and night free from other disturbances. . . . The point you make is very true: there must be no interruption" (12.9.64 HGL 60).

In 1965, the published letters of Thomas Merton make no less than seventeen references to his becoming a hermit. It was during that year that he was finally given permission by the abbot and the monastic council to move there full time. The first reference in that year is found in his February correspondence with Daniel Berrigan.

> It is definite that I am to be allowed a chance to try a crack at real hermit life. . . . Meanwhile I am in the cottage a lot more, and actually living pretty much as a hermit right now, except to come down for work in the novitiate and for some of the offices. I know I can cook, anyway. So provided enough cans of beans are sent my way, I can probably survive. No worry on that score. Gets pretty cold out there in zero weather. One thing is sure is that most of the statements made about the solitary life are sheer nonsense. I can't think of anything less likely to make a person indifferent to other people. Quite the contrary. I think that the business of herding people together is what makes them hate and misunderstand each other, or teaches them indifference. (2.26.65 HGL 86)

By May, Merton seemed certain that the move would take place, but he was unclear about just what being a hermit would mean insofar as relationships with other persons was concerned. As he wrote to Etta Gullick:

> . . . I do not know what my own position in the future will be. I have for a long time wanted to try the hermit life and it looks as if I can finally get permission for it, but naturally there will be conditions, and I probably will not be allowed to have visitors.

> We shall see. I do not mean of course that I would be leaving
> here, but living in a cottage in the woods, and as a matter of
> fact I am already spending a great deal of time there and sleep-
> ing there at night. (5.5.65 HGL 370)

The Trappist's question about being required to live in isolation
in the hermitage was also raised again in correspondence with
Berrigan: "I guess my visits are now really at an end. This is
good and bad, but anyway good from the viewpoint that I am
moving out of the novitiate and into the hermitage next month
sometime. . . . but I am pretty sure visits will more or less
completely end . . ." (5.18.65 HGL 87). At the same time he
wrote in a similar vein to his Anglican friend A. M. Allchin:
"It seems that I am going to be living permanently in the hermitage, in fact practically am now. This is a great cause for
rejoicing but it does mean that I will not be seeing people,
except perhaps rarely and exceptionally" (5.22.65 HGL 27).
As a matter of fact, once Merton moved to the hermitage his
visitors seemed to increase, given the freedom he had living
out in the woods away from the monastery. While he desired
silence and solitude, his vocation and his personality also demanded solidarity with others.

Over the years Fr. Louis became more and more convinced
of the necessity of silence and solitude, not only for himself
but for all persons. As he wrote to Etta Gullick in June of 1965:

> The more I see of it, the more I realize the absolute primacy and
> necessity of silent, hidden, poor, apparently fruitless prayer.
> The whole monastic order is being swept with currents and
> backwashes of activism and anxiety over ways to make mo-
> nasticism "count" in the modern world. The very fact that
> monks should be anxious about such things is already a strange
> symptom. However, it is balanced by the fact, as you say, that
> there are still very many who are drawn to the silent and soli-
> tary way which is really that of the monk. I think that this is
> one of the most encouraging things in Anglicanism, even
> though there is the honest-to-God set driving full speed away
> from center. (6.9.65 HGL 371)

This was a reference to the book by Anglican bishop John A. T. Robinson, titled *Honest to God*, which created a stir in the 1960s by questioning the traditional ways of understanding and speaking about the deity.

By July of 1965 the Trappist was informed by Dom James Fox that he could resign his responsibilities as novice master and move to the hermitage very soon. Merton wrote about his enthusiasm for the impending change in life to W. H. Ferry:

> This [hermitage] is what I came here for, and I think it will be, as it already has been, very fruitful. I realize that I am extremely fortunate to be able to do exactly what I am supposed to do in life: a thing which few people ever manage to get around to doing, and there is something pretty wonderful about it. I hope to continue writing, of course, in a leisurely way . . . (7.20.65 HGL 222)

Father Louis walked out of the Abbey of Gethsemani on August 22, 1965, and climbed to his new home in the woods of Mount Olivet. He spoke of this at that time as "a life without care." Thus he began to live his vocation as a Trappist monk-hermit. In a letter a few days later to Etta Gullick, he described his new life with idealism and enthusiasm—if not also a bit of romanticism. He seemed absolutely certain that he had finally found his true vocation. And he began a series of negative comments about communal life in the monastery at Gethsemani.

> Life in a hermitage is really extraordinary. As you know I had been half in and half out for almost a year, but it is quite another matter to be here all the time, with no other responsibilities, and going down only once a day. I still have to say Mass at the monastery so I go down about mid-morning, say Mass, get one cooked meal, and pick up whatever I need, then come back to the hermitage. Even when I go down I seldom have any occasion to speak to anyone, just nod to a few people and come back. Really there is no question that this does something quite tremendous for the life of prayer. It enables things to open up,

and also lets the trials get a good hold. I feel I am learning a whole new way of life, and it is really like being born again in a way. Certainly one of the things that strikes me most about it is that it is not at all what the opponents of eremitism always accuse it of being: a sort of vague life of abstraction and self-centeredness. Actually it is much less self-centered and abstract than the sort of drifting existence of irresponsibility one can get into in the community. I think that it is also far less petty. One has to be constantly concerned to do things well and do them in a manner that fits the life and the place. One certainly cannot trifle with a hermit vocation, I can see that. . . .

I can see that the real hermit life quickly brings one to precisely that kind of poverty and keeps one there. The business of being in direct dependence on God all the time is the key. Do keep me in your prayers, as the life is not easy. (8.26.65 HGL 372–73)

In his first month as a hermit Fr. Louis began to realize some of the drastic changes that are required when one lives in greater solitude and silence away from the routines of community life. As he wrote to John Wu: "If there is one truth I have learned about the hermit life, it is certainly this: that hermits are terrible letter writers" (9.12.65 HGL 631). He also wrote to Ferry with delight of his withdrawal from living like bees in "hives" in the monastery. ". . . All I can say about the life in the cottage is that it makes immense sense, and does not necessarily imply any kind of serious break with reality: quite the contrary, I am back in touch with it. Certainly a most healthy and peaceful existence, lots going on . . . I am convinced that most of man's troubles come from his illusion that he can only live in hives" (9.20.65 HGL 222–23).

By October, Merton was finding that eremitical existence made more and more sense to him. At the same time, he reflected that institutional monasticism seemed to make less and less sense—at least for him. He compared his eremitical life with his past experiences of community life in a letter to Linda Sabbath.

. . . I have obtained permission to live as a hermit in more or less complete solitude. I go to the monastery once a day for Mass and a meal, and I give one conference a week to the novices, otherwise I see no one. I am in the woods, on a hill, in a nice location with a good view, have a lot of time for meditation and prayer, but I also have manual work to do, keeping the place up, chopping wood, etc., and then I do some writing each day . . . I like the life enormously and I am convinced that this is one kind of answer to the question of how to approach the real fundamentals of the inner life. To begin with, though this is customarily regarded as a withdrawal, it is not that at all. I find the life much more real, much more in contact with actual concrete realities and facts, than life in the community, which is full of ideological baggage and all kinds of stylized and formalized activity. I also quite frankly think that life here in the woods is much more "normal" than the life most people live in the cities, all city propaganda to the contrary. Of course it is true that it can be lonely and that if one does not have the right disposition and vocation the life could be completely sterile. Actually I have found it so far immensely fruitful in every way.

The monastic Orders in the Catholic Church are in fact discovering that without this opening toward a more solitary life their own communal monasticism will remain to a great extent sterile, or just "busy." (10.3.65 HGL 519)

In November the new hermit wrote another glowing description of his experience in the woods to Marco Pallis, an English scholar of Tibetan monasticism. He called this the beginning of his "vanaprastha," and he hoped that it would be a "definitive" peeling off of many things.

I have been at it three months, and it is a splendid form of life. But three months have taught me many things and show me that I have more to learn, in order to get on the way without ambiguities. Well, that is what solitude is for and I am learning to be patient with the long task of gradually peeling off nonessential things. One would like to do it all at once but it is not possible, for various reasons. . . .

> . . . Life at the hermitage is peaceful and assumes a clear direction. One sees the way more clearly, and as you say, it is a great help to know that there are companions here and there. There is nothing whatever of any importance except this quest for inner truth, the truth that one "is" without being able to see it because we have all covered it over with the results of our selfish and deluded acts. The enormity of the task is great, yet simple, and one may have great desire and great hope of going on with the help of the Holy Spirit, in finding the path by His light in darkness. The path that leads home to Him in ourself, and the path which is also Himself. ("I am the way, the truth and the life.")
>
> I must follow my way by staying in one solitary place . . . (11.14.65 HGL 472)

Merton realized, as he wrote to Pallis a few days later, that "there have been things to be peeled off, contacts and implications in the world, especially a difficult one I was caught in with the peace movement" (12.5.65 HGL 473).

Writing in that same November to Daniel Berrigan, Merton took a somewhat more realistic, concerned, and cautious tone about the potential dangers of his new eremitical experiences.

> I don't think you have any idea what a distorted and kooky picture of things I have been getting here. . . .
>
> . . . It is bound up chiefly with the particular problems of my own life, living now my third month in more or less complete solitude (going down to the monastery for Mass and a meal and often seeing hardly anyone, let alone talking to anyone). . . . One of the things about living alone is that you suddenly find yourself thinking, perfectly plausibly, thoughts that turn out to be in themselves schizoid. It is not that one is nuts, but the situation of removal from reality and contact does that. This poses a real problem, and in order to cope with it one has to get pretty simply organized and stick with rather rudimentary and well-united elements in one simple picture. And work with that. The fact that I have always been so spread out and so scattered does present a problem. . . .

. . . I am just trying to get my own life organized in such a way that I can cope with it and do what God seems to be asking of me. This may mean throwing out very many things that don't fit. . . . I am pretty sure that I have outlived my active usefulness and that I can serve you much better by being a halfway decent hermit. (11.19.65 HGL 88)

Some of the more difficult realities of living in solitude began to be apparent to Merton by early December. He was considering backing off from his engagements with social reform movements. Visits from outsiders had been discontinued by his superiors in order to give the experiment a good try, as he wrote to Jewish rabbi and theologian Abraham Heschel: "The solitary life I find very fruitful and in some ways disconcerting. It has brought me face to face with things I had never had to consider before, and I find that some pretty drastic revaluations [?] have to be made, in my own life. This keeps me busy" (12.6.65 HGL 435). He sensed that his involvement in some of the political movements would be halted. As he wrote to Sergius Bolshakoff at the same time:

. . . while everything goes well in the hermitage I still have to break off contacts with some rather active groups in the world which are still using my name. . . . You are perfectly right that I have no further need to be writing on these topics that have a political aspect. . . .

I suppose that it will take a little time for this appearance of "engagement" in such movements to fade away. But I am at peace in the forest here in any case, and I see more and more that there is but one thing necessary. The exterior silence of the forest makes interior silence at once imperative and easy . . . (12.8.65 HGL 106)

Four letters dated in mid-to-late December of 1965 reflect his awareness that greater withdrawal from the struggles of the world meant greater struggles with his own inner world as a hermit. To social activist and theologian James Douglass he wrote: ". . . as a hermit I am no longer in a position to make political judgments in matters of detail myself. . . . Things of a general nature I suppose I can try to speak about . . ." (12.14.65 HGL 163). To Linda Sabbath, he wrote:

> After four months in the hermitage, I realize that it is necessary for me to really reorganize my whole life . . . I simply cannot carry on the nonsense of having a rather elaborate social self, professorial, guru-like, poetic, political, whatever you wish. Nuts to all of it. It simply does not fit. . . . When I was down in the monastery I had, and rightly, a quite different view of this. In my opinion, as long as I was in the monastery it would have been right and good for me not only to participate in these things by sending papers, but I should have gone myself. I think it was foolish that I was not able to do so. But up here in the woods matters are entirely different, and there is no reason whatever for me to be anything but what I am here. (12.17.65 HGL 522)

In a letter to Canadian psychiatrist Raymond Prince, the monk looked back from the vantage point of his hermitage with some negativity on his experience of monastic community: "I notice, living as a hermit, that monastic community life permits a kind of communal narcissism which siphons it all off into community projects and a sort of communal awareness which is nevertheless centered in the self multiplied (rather than in real interpersonal love). In solitude one confronts narcissism in its brute form, and either resists or succumbs completely" (12.18.65 HGL 495). Yet at the same time, to Archbishop George Flahiff of Toronto, Merton wrote quite positively of his new life: "For my own part I have been living as a hermit in the woods for over four months now and am settling down at it. It is an amazing life, and it certainly empties one out. At times I am a little dazed by it, and I can see one needs enormous grace to keep at it. But I think God asks this of me and I hope I can fully respond . . ." (12.30.65 HGL 249).

In the early months of 1966, Merton wrote to several correspondents in glowing terms about his life in the hermitage while continuing to contrast it with his years in the monastery. To William Johnston, a Jesuit scholar of spirituality living in Japan: "I am finding the hermit life very profitable indeed. The mere fact of silence and solitude is most beneficial, added to the other factor of time. It gets better as it goes on and one begins to get rid of some of the outer coverings" (1.10.66 HGL 441). To his German psychologist friend Erich Fromm, to whom he had written many times about his desire for greater solitude in the monastic life:

> . . . I have moved out of the monastery to live in the woods as a hermit . . . As to the solitary life, it is to my mind a very valid experiment. It seems to me at any rate much more serious and in some ways more exacting than the life in community, where relationships are to some extent stereotyped anyway. I use a bit of Zen out here too, though I am not cracking my head with it. It is a good life, a bit chilly at the moment . . . (1.15.66 HGL 322)

And to Jesuit Daniel Berrigan, who was always having his own difficulties with his "establishment," Merton wrote:

> For my part I can see after six months that the hermit life is anything but a hermit idea. It is a life with its own kind of problems and benefits, sometimes bitter and disillusioning, but something I cannot doubt as being what I need: it is so much more to the point than anything I ever ran into in the community, and above all it is good to get out from under the stifling mentality of the establishment . . . (2.14.66 HGL 91)

In March, Merton wrote to Marco Pallis about some of the early lessons he had learned in the hermitage. It was proving more difficult than he had anticipated, yet he was convinced of the value of pursuing the solitary, contemplative life—both for himself and for the whole church.

> In solitude I have seen more and more that everything depends on obedience to God's will and the submission of a total and uncompromising faith. This for me at the moment comes down

to the full acceptance of and adjustment to the particular situation He has willed for me here. I think that I am learning not to chafe at limitations that could objectively seem quite unreasonable, but which certainly have a purpose in my life. Spiritually I am much more free in the solitary life, but materially the limitations remain and from certain points of view they are perhaps a little cramping. Correspondence is inspected, contacts which seem valuable are liable to be abruptly cut off without my knowledge, etc. . . . I do not chafe at such things and I find in them a certain freedom of indifference, realizing that such material limitations are really unimportant and that they never prevent anything that is really willed by God. I hope that it is in the area of this higher freedom we will always be at one. . . .

Returning to the original point, of the need for an earnest life of solitude in the Catholic Church: popularly the trend seems to be in the other direction: all is action, liturgy and a thousand new projects and ideas. I think there is a great deal of good in a lot of it, and that some of it is very superficial and quite deceptive. This is another reason for a real contemplative life, not one that is half stifled by organization but one that is really lived in contact with reality and with life, in solitude. I can see that this is my real work and I certainly need to go about it in the right way. I am quite conscious of my own fallibility. (3.11.66 HGL 474–75)

March 1966 was the month that brought the first major crisis for Thomas Merton in his new existence as a hermit. His "fallibility" came to the fore as never before. The crisis began with his trip to a hospital in Louisville, about which he wrote to Etta Gullick: "I have to go to the hospital for a back operation. I hope it comes out all right, because my ability to chop wood next winter will very much depend on it. I like winter in the woods, spring even better. The life is fine but there is not much to be said about it. Writing letters is not easy. I have less and less inclination to or facility in talk" (3.8.66 HGL 375).

In the hospital, following his surgery, the fifty-year-old Trappist monk fell in love with a student nurse, a woman in her mid-twenties. His published letters over the next few months, while not mentioning this relationship explicitly, reflect some of the growing tensions that this woman brought into his hermit life and his celibate monastic commitment. This can be noted in his Holy Saturday 1966 letter to Daniel Berrigan: "I have a kind of feeling that the Abbot is using the hermit pitch as a pretext for imposing complete silence as regards not only events but even basic principles. However, I think I can always manage to say anything I really need to say" (HGL 92). One can also read an April letter to Erich Fromm as an allusion to his "illusions and desires" regarding the relationship with the woman: "Am temporarily not sleeping in the hermitage, as I am recovering from an operation for cervical disk. But I work and meditate there in the daytime when possible. Be sure that I am not exaggerating this project or being fanatical about it; but I need this delving into reality, this sweating out of illusions and desires . . . (4.27.66 HGL 322).

The next two months found the hermit reflecting on the emptiness that becomes love in solitude. It is interesting that he specifically connects love and the solitary life as he struggles with his friendship with "M." Interesting too that he wrote of this to a laywoman, Linda Sabbath, to whom he had written of his hospital stay in early April: "Here I get a great deal of tender love and care from student nurses, and the rest of the time lay around reading Meister Eckhart" (4.7.66 HGL 528). Merton continued his correspondence with Sabbath:

> Not much point in longing for solitude, it is not something you get but something you have. It is you. What are you looking for? To see yourself as a happy object? It is a waste of time. Being solitary, I no longer give it a thought, because solitude is an illusion like everything else. The only ground is emptiness, which is love. And this is not something we generate under nice and favorable conditions. The conditions are unimportant. (5.14.66 HGL 529)

Two weeks later the hermit wrote again to Sabbath about the hermitage leading him to face the realities of his life.

I am back in the hermitage completely now, sleeping and all. It is a big relief to get back, it is my natural habitat and that is what counts. All is not simple and easy in the solitary life, but the thing about it is that the trials make sense and one sees that one has to go through them and put up with them, and one tries to meet it all in a constructive sort of way. So it is work to do. (5.26.66 HGL 529)

Apparently Sabbath responded by asking Merton to explain what he meant by the difficulties he was experiencing in the solitary life. He replied at length in June—again without specifically mentioning his relationship with the nurse:

"All is not easy and simple in the solitary life." This is no mysterious statement. It simply means what it says, and is quite clear to anyone who has ever read anything about it, or been involved in it. It is an unusual life in which one has to find out a great deal by trial and error and in which there are few really valid road maps because each vocation is different, each situation is different, each one has in himself his own devils to fight with. . . .

Actually, I don't say my life is crawling with problems. I have far fewer real problems in the hermitage that are specifically hermitage problems than I had in the community. I would not change the life for anything. I am not going around singing alleluias about how beautiful it is, because by now I am used to it and don't especially want to talk about it. I am not going to write much at all about solitude because when I am living it that is enough, there is no point in watching myself live it. I turn my mind to something else when it comes to speaking out. It is simply the only life I am at all ready to live seriously and for keeps. The rest does not interest me for five seconds. I lay no claims at all to being a first-class hermit or a first-class anything else. But I know this silence and this aloneness in the woods is for me: that's the best I can say about it. As to being the one who is going to make the road maps: sorry. I guess if that is needed someone will come along and do it. In any case my own solitude is quite peculiar because I am a writer and hence there are modalities in it which are not those of an "ordinary" hermit vocation, if such a thing exists. No hermit is ordinary. We are all cracked in slightly different ways, that's all. The first thing is to accept ourselves as we are and God's grace as it is given (to learn to recognize this, one may need help, I guess), and then learn to live without too many exorbitant plans and projects for the future. To do this now is already a good preparation for the solitary life, I think. It constitutes a kind of desert existence that has a validity of its own . . . (6.18.66 HGL 530)

One of hermit Merton's concerns was his diet. He did not like to waste time cooking and would usually bring simple foods from the monastery to his hermitage. He wrote of these issues to Sabbath in 1966:

> I would say that food has always been one of my big problems around here, because after a few years I became allergic to milk products. For a long time I did quite well on rice and eggs (and of course other vegetables). Now I am supposed to eat in the infirmary refectory, where they give me meat. But in fact none of the food they give there interests me at all. It is nothing but industrialized canned stuff, tasteless and even repugnant, and as a result I have been eating little, which is perhaps a good thing. In the hermitage my eating habits are terrible: I will eat cans of sardines and potato chips. I am convinced that food is very important in the life of meditation. (7.9.66 HGL 531)

It is interesting that Thomas Merton's letters about being a hermit during the summer of 1966—when he was working through the complexities of his relationship with "M"—are written mainly to a laywoman. Perhaps he needed the female ear to bounce things off during those months. In July he wrote again to Sabbath, going into some detail about his daily routines in the hermitage. The note of anxiety about his "problems" seems not to be so noticeable at that time.

> I just don't want to get involved in a lot of cooking in the hermitage, it takes up valuable time that could be used sitting around looking at the birds.

> In the hermitage I have the things that can be of most im-
> mediate use to me here, things like the various spreads for
> sandwiches, etc., the rose tea or whatever it is, and the dried
> bananas, the medicines and that . . .
>   . . . I eat little in the hermitage and a very little bit goes a
> long way.
>   . . . There is no question that I need to be more rational about
> what I eat. We all do here. (7.19.66 HGL 531)

In August he wrote to Etta Gullick of his happiness in being
in the hermitage and away from monastery routines. He was
living by his own natural contemplative rhythm out in the
woods.

> . . . I got back into the hermitage in the middle of May. It is the
> best place for me, though I may have it hard in winter. But now
> I sleep here better than anywhere else, and of course I am happy
> to have the early-morning hours up here where it is quiet, for
> meditation, reading and so on. I doubt if I could ever adjust
> happily to the monastery schedule now. I am so used to this
> one here. I never find it boring, and there is always plenty to
> do. (8.1.66 HGL 376)

Perhaps it was his working through his commitment to
monastic life and being a hermit along with his friendship with
the nurse that prompted his writing to Dorothy Day that fall.
"When one is entirely on his own, I find that curious mistakes
become possible. But with the guidance of grace and normal
good will they do not have effects that are too terrible" (9.12.66
HGL 152).

Having passed through the most difficult part of his rela-
tional and vocational crisis by the fall of 1966, Thomas Merton
wrote three quite similar letters reflecting the peace he was
experiencing in his one-year-old hermit life. To Erich Fromm:

> . . . I am thriving in the hermitage: it is the ideal milieu for me,
> out in the woods, plenty of silence and inner freedom. I am not

cut off in an artificial way from other people . . . Really I feel
much more human and natural on my own than when tied up
in the routines of an institution. Here I don't have to play any
part at all, and that is very delightful. I just live. (10.13.66
HGL 324)

To Abraham Heschel: "I am, as you know, happily holed away
in the woods where I belong and find the existence perfectly
congenial. I could not ask for anything better, and in snow it is
even quieter still . . ." (12.12.66 HGL 436). And to Abdul Aziz:

> My life in the hermitage continues to be quiet and simple. In
> fact I find that I can no longer carry on the same kind of routines
> as I did before. . . . I find it almost impossible to write about
> more or less personal matters, I seem to have nothing whatever
> to say. . . . My time in the hermitage is divided between study
> and meditation. Since the operation I have not been able to do
> much manual work. The silence of the woods is perfect. I go to
> the monastery once or twice a day but not for long. (12.28.66
> HGL 64–65)

After allowing himself the experiences of interpersonal love,
monk Merton seemed to realize more than ever that he shared
a common humanity with everyone, especially his friends
who, like himself, found themselves "in the thick of things."
Merton had come to describe his "church" as his friends and
colleagues. He wrote of this twice during the spring of 1967 to
his friend Amiya Chakravarty. "May we all grow in grace and
peace, and not neglect the silence that is printed in the center
of our being. It will not fail us. It is more than silence. Jesus
spoke of the spring of living water, you remember . . ." (4.13.67
HGL 116). And again:

> Living alone in the woods, I am more appreciative of friendship
> than ever before. . . .
>   . . . I am human enough to want to see the people I have
> come to know through you . . . (4.25.67 HGL 116)

Some of Merton's most extensive and personal reflections on his life as a hermit can be found in his correspondence of spring and summer 1967, with theologian Rosemary Radford Ruether. Writing in February he reflected on some of his midlife questions about his vocation and the style of his living the monastic quest.

> In other words I have the usual *agonia* with my vocation but now, after twenty-five years, I am in a position where I am practically laicized and de-institutionalized, and living like all the other old bats who live alone in the hills in this part of the country and I feel like a human being again. My hermit life is expressly a *lay* life. I never wear the habit except when at the monastery and I try to be as much on my own as I can and like the people around the country. Also I try as best I can to keep up valid and living contacts with my friends who are in the thick of things, and everyone knows where my real "community" is. I honestly believe that is the right place for me (woods, not Gethsemani) insofar as it is the right battleground. It is a sort of guerrilla-outpost type of thing if you like. But from my experience I would myself be leading a less honest and more faked life if I were back in the cities. This is no reflection on anyone else. In staying here I am not just being here for myself but for my friends, my Church, and all those I am one with. Also, if there is one thing I am sure of too, it is my need to fight out in my own heart whatever sort of fight for honesty I have to wage and for fidelity to God. I am not by any means turning my back on other people, I am as open as the situation (of overcontrol) permits and want to make this more open as time goes on. Lots of people would like me to get out and join them in this or that, but I just don't see that I could do it without getting into some absurd role and having to act a dumb part or justify some nonsense or other that I don't really believe in. I know I firmly disbelieve all the favorite clichés about monasticism, and the community knows it too. I can't say where and how my life is eschatological, because as far as I can see I am a tramp and not much else. But this kind of tramp is what I am supposed to be. This kind of place is where I am finally reduced to my nothingness and have to depend on God. Outside I would

be much more able to depend on talk. Maybe I am just protesting too much, but that is the way I feel about it. I assure you
that whatever else it is it is not complacency, because there is
ample material for not being complacent, I assure you . . .
(2.14.67 HGL 501–2)

Ruether wrote in early March that she was ". . . radically
out of sympathy with the monastic project, not merely in its
fallen state, but also in its original and most intrinsic self-
understanding" (Mary Tardiff, ed., *At Home in the World*, 27).
She judged monasticism to be a withdrawal from the world
that ". . . always was a misunderstanding of the Gospel" (28).
She protested that salvation is meant to be "of" the world, not
"from" the world. She said strongly of Merton's monastic vocation: "You have not withdrawn from this world into heaven,
you have withdrawn from creation into hell!" While acknowl-
edging that contemplation could be an "auxiliary help" in
serving the world, it was not to become an end in itself (29).
She wished that ". . . monasticism could view itself as a ministry, as a place to which the whole church could have recourse
as a place of contemplation, but contemplation for the sake of
the main area of salvation which takes place precisely in the
sphere of historical action . . ." (30).
Merton replied with a characteristic honesty and clarity that
confronted Ruether's position head-on, especially as a defense
of his call to the hermitage.

Honestly, your view of monasticism is to me so abstract and so
in a way arbitrary (though plenty of basis in texts can be found)
that it is simply poles apart from the existential, concrete,
human dimension which the problem has for us here. . . . Let
me put it this way: I am so far from being "an ascetic" that I
am in many ways an antiascetic humanist, and one of the things
in monasticism that has always meant most to me is that monastic life is in closer contact with God's good creation and is
in many ways simpler, saner and more human than life in the
supposedly comfortable, pleasurable world. One of the things
I love about my life, and therefore one of the reasons why I would

not change it for anything, is the fact that I live in the woods and according to a tempo of sun and moon and season in which it is naturally easy and possible to walk in God's light, so to speak, in and through his creation. That is why the narcissist bit in prayer and contemplation is no problem out here, because in fact I seldom have to fuss with any such thing as "recollecting myself" and all that rot. All you do is breathe, and look around. And wash dishes, type, etc. Or just listen to the birds. I say this in all frankness, realizing that I can be condemned for having it so much better than almost anybody. That is what I feel guilty about, I suppose, but certainly not that I have repudiated God's good creation. Sure, it is there in the cities too, but in such a strained, unnatural, tense shape . . . Absolutely the last thing in my own mind is the idea that the monk de-creates all that God has made. On the contrary, monks are, and I am, in my own mind, the remnant of desperate conservationists. . . . In a word, to my mind the monk is one of those who not only saves the world in the theological sense but saves it literally, protecting it against the destructiveness of the rampaging city of greed, war, etc. And this loving care for natural creatures becomes, in some sense, a warrant of his theological mission and ministry as a man of contemplation. . . .

. . . [This is] an example of what I myself am doing in my "secularized" existence as hermit. I am not only leading a more "worldly" life (me and the rabbits), but am subtly infecting the monastery with worldly ideas. I still am requested to give one talk a week in community, and have covered things like Marxism and the idea of dialogue à la Garaudy, Hromadka and so on, and especially all kinds of literary material, Rilke for some time, and now for a long time a series of lectures on Faulkner and his theological import. This is precisely what I think a hermit ought to do for the community which has seen fit deliberately and consciously to afford him liberty. I have a liberty which can fruitfully serve my brothers, and by extension I think it indicates what might be the monk's role for the rest of the Church . . . (3.9.67 HGL 502–5)

Not to be dissuaded of her views, Ruether wrote that the Trappist should be out struggling against the dehumanizing forces of the city of man, not planting trees in some romanticized agrarian dream. He replied that his was a special way of being in conversation with the *polis*:

> . . . it is not at all a question of repudiating political life but of participating in a way that makes sense here. . . . we both seem to be accepting a naive and unreal separation between "city" and "country" that no longer means anything in the modern world. . . .
>
> . . . Certainly the demons down here are small-time. But it is by confronting them that a monk has to open the way to his own kind of involvement in the big-time struggle . . . to be effectively iconoclastic in the modern world. . . . I am in the most uncomfortable and unenviable position of waiting without any justification, without a convincing explanation, and without any assurance except that it seems to be what God wants of me and that this kind of desperation is what it means for me to be without idols—I hope. . . . the monastic life can play a very helpful part in the worldly struggle precisely because of the different perspective which it has and should preserve. What is needed is for the doors to open and for people to get around more and learn a little.
>
> . . . "being a hermit" seems to mean trying to be a very peculiar and special kind of artificial man, whereas for me what it means is being nothing but man, . . . that is to say as a non-monk even, a non-layman a non-categorized man a plain simple man: not as an ideal status or a condition of "striving for spiritual perfection," but a reduction to the bare condition of man as a starting point where everything has to begin: incomplete and insufficient in the sense of being outside social cadres. But then, entering into these in a free and tentative way, in an exploratory way, to establish new and simple relationships. . . . What would seem to others to be the final step into total alienation seems to me to be the beginning of the resolution of all alienation and the preparation for a real return without masks and without defenses into the world, as mere man. (3.19.67 HGL 505–8)

The Trappist's dialogue with the theologian continued intensely through the first half of 1967. While he very much appreciated her challenges and thought the questions helped him to reframe his own answers, he continued to argue for the worldly witness value of his contemplative call. He did, however, write less and less on this point. In March he wrote of questioning the survival of the shape of monasticism as it existed at Gethsemani:

> . . . one reason why the Abbot so easily consented in letting me be a hermit is that this gives him extra leverage: "Hermits never travel." (Which is pure crap: hermits are the most traveling of all Christians.)
>
> All this outcry about freedom.
>
> Refusal to grapple with the idea of monastic renewal because I see that too much is really involved, and that what is going on here now is superficial: what is really in question is the survival of the kind of thing we have here. They are trying to save it, or at least the general structure. I realize obscurely that it can't be saved, has to be entirely rebuilt from the bottom up . . . (3.25.67 HGL 510)

Despite the fact that in 1967, Merton was questioning the viability of the institution of monasticism as it then existed, in April he still defended the value of his own monkish witness for the world. Admittedly it is, however, a great mystery, beyond clear demonstration. As he wrote to Ruether, ". . . I don't think I am rationalizing or evading when I say I think I owe it to you to pursue my own way and stand on my own in this sort of marginal and lost position I have. I am sometimes terribly hit by its meaning which is something I just cannot explain, because it is something you are not supposed to explain and must get along without explaining" (4.9.67 HGL 511).

For Merton the hermit life was lived in ever deepening communion of love and compassion with the whole world. ". . . a hermit today is not all that isolated, with letters, planes coming down this way, and so on. I think I am probably much more in communication with people all over the place, all over the world, than most active lifers are. So much for the treetop: but I don't deny the water sounds fine where you are . . ." (Ruether, 5.5.67 HGL 511).

While not being attached to labels regarding religious life, Merton wanted the freedom to witness in his own unique way to the contemplative critique of life in the world.

> . . . What I do absolutely agree with is the need to be free from a sort of denominational tag. Though I have one in theory (people still have me categorized in terms of The Seven Storey Mtn) I am really not any of the things they think, and I don't comfortably wear the label of monk either, because I am now convinced that the first way to be a decent monk is to be a non-monk and an anti-monk, as far as the "image" goes: but I am certainly quite definite about wanting to stay in the bushes (provided I can make some sort of noises that will reach my offbeat friends) . . . (Ruether, 5.5.67 HGL 511)

By July the hermit could still stand firm in his commitment to witness from the woods, no matter how unreal it may seem to others.

> . . . So for my part, even though it is only a gesture and largely unreal (obviously I am not one of the hillbillies), I hang on in desperation to what I think I have been called to, trusting not in it but in the mercy of Christ, who knows better than I that it isn't real, but that it is at least a choice. And there don't seem to be more meaningful ones around, for me, all things considered. (Ruether, 7.17.67 HGL 513)

By that time, the hermitage had become quite "real" for Merton as a man of sacramental faith since he had begun to celebrate Eucharist there on a regular basis, as he wrote to Sr. M. Emmanuel, a Brazilian religious: "I enjoy the quiet of the hermitage and am saying Mass here now, which is very beautiful at least for me. I did not realize it would mean so much. I have two authentic ikons over my altar, one Bulgarian and one Greek, both from good periods, and also two good copies of Russian ikons" (7.31.67 HGL 199). He wrote in a similar, somewhat bucolic vein to Christopher Mwoleka: ". . . I am now able to live in the woods about ten minutes' walk from the monastery. It is quite a solitary place and no one comes here. The arrangement is good, as I can get the food I need from the monastery, and go there for one meal a day. The rest of the time I am here. I continue of course to work, writing and so on" (9.13.67 HGL 462).

Near the second anniversary of Merton's move into the hermitage, he wrote to Dorothy Day about the spiritual struggles which had surfaced for him as he lived in solitude. His reflections indicate a lessening of his initial rather romantic views of living alone in the woods.

> . . . The hermit life is no joke at all, and no picnic, but in it one gradually comes face to face with the awful need of self-emptying and even of a kind of annihilation so that God may be all, and also the apparent impossibility of it. And of course the total folly of trying to find ways of doing it oneself. The great comfort is in the goodness and sweetness and nearness of all God has made, and the created isness which makes Him first of all present in us, speaking us. Then that other word: "Follow . . ." (8.18.67 HGL 152–53)

The following month, again to Day, Merton expressed his joy in the experience of solitude and silence in the hermitage. "The solitude that has been granted me here is certainly a precious gift and I value it most highly. The long hours of complete silence are the best thing in the world and I appreciate them more than I can say. Pray that I use them well!" (9.19.67 HGL 153).

Not long after that Thomas Merton wrote to Abdul Aziz about how he was spending his silent, solitary hours. It is evident that he was, indeed, learning to "use them well!"

> First, it is true that one who is learning to meditate must also learn to get along without any support external to his own heart and the gifts of God. Hence it is good for such a one to have to remain in silence without reading or even using vocal prayers sometimes, in order to come to terms with the need for inner

struggle and discipline. On the other hand this is not a universal rule. There are times when it is necessary to read, and even to read quite a lot, in order to store up material and get new perspectives. In the solitary life, however, though one has a lot of time for reading, it becomes difficult to read a great deal. One finds that in a couple of hours he reads only a few pages. The rest of the time is spent in reflection and prayer. It becomes difficult to absorb more than this. Someone in solitude who would read voraciously all the time might perhaps be considered in the wrong place. Moderate reading is, however, normal. Provided that more time is spent in prayer and meditation than in reading . . . (1.16.68 HGL 66)

January of 1968 brought great changes to the Abbey of Gethsemani and to the life of Thomas Merton. Dom James Fox resigned after nineteen years as abbot. Fox had fought hard in Cistercian circles to allow experimentation with the hermit life in their Order. Interestingly, after leaving office, he, like Merton, entered a rather elaborate hermitage that Fox had had constructed at some greater distance from the abbey than Merton's.

Merton had long been frustrated by the regime of Dom James. Under this abbot who held a degree from Harvard Business School, he judged that the monastery had become too much of a successful business operation. It was too busy and too noisy to be a place for serious contemplative living. Merton also had long chafed under his abbot's restrictions on his travel, his outside contacts, and on having his letters censored.

Father Louis had written of this with irony in 1964: "Fr. Abbot would not let me accept an invitation to Japan to see the Zen people, said the higher Abbot thought that this request, coinciding with an interest in the solitary life, was a manifestation of a 'dual personality.' Meanwhile Fr. Abbot is off to Norway, for the blessing of a bishop friend. A Cistercian . . ." (Ferry, 12.5.64 HGL 220). Again in 1967 he wrote of his strong feelings regarding the limitations that were placed upon him by the long-tenured abbot. "It is perfectly true that I need to get out of here and get around a bit, and I know it only too well. This is one of the most frustrating things about the complete irrationality of my Abbot, who will not and cannot even discuss such a thing with equanimity" (Ruether, 3.24.67 HGL 509).

The resignation of Dom James was announced during the fall of 1967. In November Merton told Sr. M. Emmanuel with apparent relief and high hopes: "The Abbot is resigning. The new Abbot may be a different matter. This Abbot is obsessed with the fear of my going elsewhere and not coming back, as if that would be bad for the 'image' of Gethsemani—or bad for business, in other words. It is ludicrous, but I can't do anything about it. Give us a couple of months and things will probably be very different" (10.30.67 HGL 200).

Monk Merton also wrote to Berrigan of his hopes for greater freedom to travel under the new abbot. He remained somewhat suspicious, however, regarding the retiring abbot's continuing influence in the monastery and perhaps over his life.

> The present Abbot is retiring. No idea who the next one will be, but I want to give him every possible chance to be different. In particular I want to see if he will not be a lot more open than this one about letting me get a little more freedom of movement, which I could certainly use to advantage. . . . At the present moment, if I get involved in some public manifestation of something or other, it will unduly complicate matters and guarantee more years of doghouse, without any real need to do so. . . .
>   . . . Trouble about the Abbot who is retiring here is that he will stay around and continue to influence things indirectly. He has a very snappylooking hermitage going up on a distant hill. (11.27.67 HGL 98–99)

On January 13, 1968, Dom Flavian Burns, a fellow hermit at Gethsemani, was elected Merton's new abbot. Fr. Louis wrote with evident joy to A. M. Allchin: "We have a good new Abbot: one of the other hermits" (2.1.68 HGL 30). He gave a thumbnail description of the new abbot in a letter to W. H. Ferry a few days after the election:

> New Abbot is a very good man: young, but willing, definite, open, with solid monastic ideas not crackpot ones.
>   Old Abbot still in no hurry to rush off into the freezing woods. Is around getting his "papers together" for a few weeks. (1.25.68 HGL 237)

To Daniel Berrigan, Merton wrote in February:

> The new Abbot . . . is a real good man, perhaps the best we could expect in the circumstances . . .
>   Perhaps also I may harvest a few secondary gains going and coming, be able to see some friends, etc. (2.8.68 HGL 99)

And to Sergius Bolshakoff, Merton wrote in April of his sense of some of the changes brewing under Dom Flavian. These were changes that Merton obviously favored because there would be a greater call for solitude, silence, and a clear affirmation of hermits living within the community. "The new Fr. Abbot is intent on reducing the activity in the community and thus giving the monks more taste for a deeper contemplative life. . . . All of us here are hoping to cut down on extra activity. I myself will write less. It is of course already necessary for me to cut down on correspondence" (4.26.68 HGL 107).

In the early months of 1968, Thomas Merton had another dream come true. A chapel and an inside toilet and shower were completed at his hermitage. As he wrote to W. H. Ferry in February: "I'm having a small addition built on to my place. When the workmen get through, I hope to hole in for a good part of Lent. Then maybe I'll get a couple of things done I want to do . . ." (2.21.68 HGL 237).

Abbot Flavian was open to Merton accepting selected invitations to travel and speak outside the monastery. When Merton was invited to attend and address a conference of East and West monastics in Bangkok, Thailand, the abbot told Merton that he was free to decide whether he would go. Thus, just as Merton seemed to be settling into the hermitage—with greater creature comforts—his life began to move elsewhere.

During 1968, his final year of life, Merton's epistolary comments upon his life as a hermit were written almost exclusively to Ferry. These nine letters were in regard to Merton's anticipated trips to California, Alaska, and Asia. In May he flew to California, where he visited the Trappistine monastery in northern California and became greatly enamored of those environs. He sent a coastal picture of the area to Ferry saying: "Here (over) is a spot on the Cal. shore I am in love with. Certainly do hope to return. Kentucky is muggy and stuffy and unprepossessing right now. . . . The monastery is fine—chapel getting back in shape" (5.24.68 HGL 238).

In writing to Ferry, Thomas Merton began to imagine possibilities of establishing his hermitage there in California.

> A wonderful idea to get a place on the Pacific—too bad you aren't further north, you c'd buy Beau Harbor. But probably there are many equally fine places down at Big Sur—except I always wonder if that isn't too well known now. One very lovely place near the convent is obtainable, but lacks view of the sea. Very high up, lovely, well-protected little ranch. All around there, full of great places.
>
> I am fully set on spending any time I can on that shore and wish I could move out for keeps. (6.1.68 HGL 238)

A few days later he told Ferry: "I miss the Coast! Understatement of the year . . ." (6.6.68 HGL 239). And again, a few days later, he wrote to Ferry of his return visit to California on his way to Asia: "Well, I really do take seriously the idea of exploring the Pacific Coast with you. There is no question that I really need a top-secret hideout where nobody will know I am there and where I can be alone with a lot of wind and sea for long periods—perhaps indefinitely" (6.16.68 HGL 239).

July found the Trappist still planning his exploration of the California coast with Ferry, as a place for a possible hermitage.

"Could we think of our exploration of Pacific Coast right at beginning of November or end of October? Abbot is interested in something on Coast. I am hoping it will really develop eventually—but he might be amenable to my settling down in Cal. for a while (in isolated spot) on return from Asia—like January" (7.8.68 HGL 239).

Later in that same month the monk showed that he was becoming very specific in his mapping out the trip up the coast of northern California. As he wrote to Ferry:

> . . . my own idea would be to see as much of the actual coast as one leisurely can, probably following route 1 all the way up to Fort Bragg and then cutting over to get to Vina (near Redding).
>
> For my part I'd like to spend some of the time just sitting around on a point meditating and listening to the waves: maybe we could stop here and there and you could watch birds meanwhile. But my main objective I guess is to explore around for a possible hideaway where I could get some real solitude someday, temporarily or permanently. In other words the Abbot—Fr. Flavian—is seriously thinking of setting something up out there one day. But he seems willing to let me move out there on my own quite soon. Even this winter, when I get back from Asia. I imagine it would mean being on land near the nuns at Redwoods, or else squatting on somebody else's territory. That is the real serious intent I have in mind. Probably I'll end up in the north near the nuns, as that is the most practical thing to do (re food etc.) but it would not hurt to look at the southern coast around Lucia—Big Sur, and also perhaps get back into the Zen place at Tassajara spring and see other such places in those mts. (7.20.68 HGL 240)

As Thomas Merton was about to set out on his journey to the East, passing through both California and Alaska, he was aware that his presence in northern California could cause quite a stir in the press. He cautioned Ferry about the need for "much discretion." "Moving fast up coast fine with me. A couple of days around the ins and outs between Mendocino and Eureka good. I'm all for the desolate mists and the nords. Might be somebody in Eureka ready to give or lend an acre of sandbar or something. I'll find out, but it needs to be done with much discretion I guess, so's not to set off a great chain of firecrackers all over Cal." (9.4.68 HGL 242).

Merton first visited Alaska before coming to meet Ferry in California. There too he sought potential sites for a hermitage more remote than the one provided for him at Gethsemani. He wrote to Ferry that Alaska might prove to be the best spot. "If our exploration of California is a bit shorter, it won't affect much my original purpose because I have found enough lonely spots here in AZlaska (zow that's a grand word) to last any hermit until Judgment Day. It is quite possible that if and whenever I get back from Asia, I may end up here. . . . The mountains are the finest I have ever seen anywhere. It is a GREAT land" (9.26.68 HGL 244).

Of course, as we now sadly know, the "if" proved more real and true than the "whenever" when it came to Thomas Merton's return from Asia. He died there on December 10, 1968, of accidental electrocution. He who had sought to disappear into God did so at the early age of fifty-three. In fact, the final words of his speech that day were: "And I shall disappear." The dream of a true hermit!

8

On Interreligious Dialogue

By the late 1950s, Thomas Merton's insatiable quest for spiritual truth had led him into the study of Eastern religions. Having converted to Roman Catholicism in 1938, he never stopped searching the riches of the Christian tradition for the promised truth that would set him free. Once steeped in the Western spiritual tradition, however, the monk felt free to look toward the East for further inspiration and different expressions of the one, same truth. As he wrote to his friend John Harris in May of 1959: "You see that my concept of Christianity is far from being an old-maidish theology of hiding in a corner of the house and standing on chairs for fear of heretical mice" (5.5.59 HGL 390).

Merton was reading widely in the area of Eastern religions and philosophies at that time, and one of his early interests was the spiritual traditions of China. He discussed some of his curiosity about and appreciation of *I Ching* with Harris.

> . . . the Book of Oracles called the *I Ching* . . . consists of a
> series of symbolic configurations of events, or "changes" which
> one arrives at by drawing lots or tossing coins; but that is not
> the important thing. What is fascinating is the fact that each
> change is exactly that sort of fluid "style of movement" . . .
> "arrangement of groups" . . . which constitutes Pasternak's

inclinations. Jung has written a fascinating preface to the I Ching, bringing in his archetypes. The I Ching had a tremendous influence on both Confucius and Lao Tzu, and what amazes me is that it is exactly the Pasternak approach. . . . It can be a very disturbing book, at the wrong moment. Because of its oracular character, one has to play the game it proposes, in order to see what it is really driving at. This should not be done by one who is not clear where fortune-telling ends and analysis begins. . . . But there is always danger of setting off some kind of an interior explosion; the symbols are really powerful, and their strange conjunctions can turn out to be devastating if once we take them in some way seriously, which true understanding of the book requires. The whole subject is supremely interesting, and really beyond me, as I am not an analyst or that much of a scholar in these matters. (5.5.59 HGL 389)

Then Merton asked Harris to note the connections and similarities between East and West on so many spiritual points:

But the important thing for you at the moment is not *Zen* or *I Ching,* so please do not let me distract you from what really matters. All that these others have to teach is found in the Church also (and they too are of "the Church" in their own hidden way). There is such a sea of wonderful things for you both to fall into and swim in—where can you begin? . . .

The great thing is not things but God Himself Who is not things but ourselves, and the world, and everything, lost in Him Who so fully IS that we come closer to Him by imagining He is not. The Being of all and my own Being is a vast emptiness containing nothing: I have but to swim in it and be carried away in it to see that this nothing is All. This too may be a distracting way of putting it: but everything is really very simple and do not let yourselves be disturbed by appearances of complication and multiplicity. *Omnia in omnibus Christus.* Let His Spirit carry you where He wills, and do not be disturbed if I sometimes talk like Eckhart . . . (5.5.59 HGL 390)

Thomas Merton's principal and long-term interest in Eastern religions would appear to have been Buddhism, Zen in particular. He was writing of this to Erich Fromm as early as 1954. From his reading Merton was beginning to realize the mystics' sense of the nondualism of all reality and of the source of reality. It is interesting to note that, at this early phase in his understanding, he spoke of Buddhism as "more or less atheistic." This was a generally common view among Christian thinkers of that time.

> Jnana yoga and perhaps Buddhism are more or less atheistic, but the majority of true mystics stand or fall with the existence or nonexistence of God. Besides there is, it seems to me, the absolute ontological impossibility of anything existing if God does not exist. However, I have argued on that point long and uselessly enough not to start it again. I think what you are really saying is that true mysticism does not know God after the manner of an object, and that is perfectly true. God is not experienced as an object outside ourselves, as "another being" capable of being enclosed in some human concept. Yet though He be known as the source of our own being . . . (10.2.54 HGL 310–11)

In a 1958 correspondence with English author Aldous Huxley, the Trappist had apparently been practicing Zen sitting and was finding it to be an avenue into contemplative awareness. At this stage he speaks of it only as a "natural perfection." Later he will realize that natural and supernatural are not the most useful categories for considerations of contemplation and mysticism.

> . . . I am interested in yoga and above all in Zen, which I find to be the finest example of a technique leading to the highest *natural* perfection of man's contemplative liberty. You may argue that the use of a koan to dispose one for satori is not different from the use of a drug. I would like to submit that there is all the difference in the world . . . (11.27.58 HGL 439)

Thomas Merton was perhaps writing of his own experience with Zen meditation when he wrote to Dorothy Day in August

138 A Focus on Truth

1960 about the importance of falling into the emptiness at the center of our being, an emptiness that is our all. "We should in a way fear for our perseverance because there is a big hole in us, an abyss, and we have to fall through it into emptiness, but the Lord will catch us. Who can fall through the center of himself into that nothingness and not be appalled? But the Lord will catch us. He will catch you without fail and take you to His heart" (8.17.60 HGL 138).

Perhaps too this is something of what Merton was coming to mean by the "disinterested love" that is spoken of in mystical traditions, and of which he wrote to Kansas professor Jeanne Burdick at about the same time:

> The way I would express it now is in purely religious and symbolic terms. That we should "love God" not merely to convince ourselves that we are good people, or to get a warm glow of peace, or to fit in with an approving group, or to get rid of anxiety, but to throw all that to the winds, and anxiety or not, even though we realize the utter depth of our inadequacy, to realize that this simply does not matter in the "eyes of God" for, as we are, with our misfortunes and needs, "we are His joy" and He delights to be loved by us with perfect confidence in Him because He is love itself. This is of course not capable of being put in scientific language, it is religious symbol. But if you will be patient with it, and stay with it, I think you will find it is the most fundamental symbol and the deepest truth: at least I am trying to express that which is deepest and most essential. My own symbol may be very poor. But that is the way I would put it. It is not that we have to sweat and groan to placate an austere Father God in our own imagination, but rather to realize, with liberation and joy, that *He is not that at all.* That in fact He is none of our idols, none of our figments, nothing that we can imagine anyway, but that He is Love Itself. And if we realize this and love Him simply and purely in order to "please Him," we become as it were His "crown" and His "delight" and life itself is transformed in this light which is disinterested love. (12.26.61 HGL 109)

In 1961 Merton had the opportunity for further extensive epistolary exchanges with the great Japanese Zen Buddhist philosopher D. T. Suzuki. He was even given extraordinary permission to fly to New York in 1964 for a personal meeting with Suzuki. The monk wrote of his impressions of Suzuki to Jeanne Burdick in December 1961: "Dr. Suzuki is an interesting and splendid mind, and a great Buddhist. And I enjoyed trying to keep up with his Zen, which after all does have some parallel in the Western tradition. Disinterested love opens a way to the understanding of both" (12.26.61 HGL 110).

Nearly one year later Merton was finding more and more commonality between Buddhism and Christianity at the level of spiritual experience. He wrote to philosopher E. I. Watkin that he thought that Buddhist philosophy can be equated in some ways with St. Thomas Aquinas when it comes to understanding "being."

> . . . the true reality of the Church is precisely what the Gospel said it is: the communion of "saints" in the Holy Spirit. . . .
>
> That brings me to Buddhism. I am on and off thinking a great deal about it, when I can, because I think in many ways it is very germane and close to our own approaches to inner truth in Christ. Naturally, I am glad to find myself in the company of such a man as Don Chapman, in being called a Buddhist, because that is one of the standard jokes in the community here: that I am a hermit and a Buddhist and that in choir I am praying as a Buddhist (how do they know?), while others are all wrapped up in the liturgical movement and in getting the choir on pitch and in manifesting togetherness, whatever that is. Really I do not feel myself in opposition with anyone or with any form of spirituality, because I no longer think in such terms at all: this spirituality is *the* right kind, that is *the* wrong kind, etc. Right sort and wrong sort: these are sources of delusion in the spiritual life and there precisely is where the Buddhists score, for they bypass all that. Neither this side of the stream nor on the other side: yet one must cross the stream and thrown away the boat, before seeing that the stream wasn't there. . . .

Even philosophically, however, I have a sneaking suspicion that what Buddhism is getting at is by no means a Platonic absolute, abstract, but right at the heart of the concrete *act of being* which is the great intuition of Thomism (not of "the Thomists," from whom may God deliver us). I should perhaps have said "of St. Thomas" . . . (11.15.62 HGL 580)

Buddhism is sometimes criticized by theists as being purely philosophical or psychological. Merton commented on this in a letter to Etta Gullick in March 1963: "I think there is a lot to be learned from the Buddhists, as regards the natural and psychological side of contemplation, especially some of the most obvious psychological blocks, which we blithely ignore, and to our cost" (3.24.63 HGL 359).

By 1963 Thomas Merton's principal focus in interreligious study was clearly Buddhism, and Zen in particular. As he wrote to Tibetan religious scholar Marco Pallis in July:

To my mind the meeting of Eastern and Western philosophy and mysticism is a crucially important matter. My general feeling is that the work that has been done so far, and the kind of thing I myself might be able to participate in, is not thorough enough and too intuitive. Of course a sapiential approach must be intuitive. But a great deepening is necessary. The task of getting to know the Eastern literature thoroughly is immense, and I do not have any Oriental languages. I might say, however, that I have a deep affinity and respect for Buddhism, and I think that I am as much a Chinese Buddhist in temperament and spirit as I am a Christian. I don't find any contradiction in matters of "faith" as I see it. But of course I say this without having an expert knowledge of the literature, and perhaps it is only irresponsibility and impressionism. I think one can certainly believe in the revealed truths of Christianity and follow Christ, while at the same time having a Buddhist outlook on life and nature. Or in other words, a certain element of Buddhism in culture and spirituality is by no means incompatible with Christian belief . . . (HGL 464–65)

In 1964 Merton was asked to write a report on Buddhist literature for the Cistercian magazine *Collectanea Cisterciana*. To prepare for that project he wrote to William Johnston, SJ, at Sophia University in Japan, in order to increase his grasp of Buddhism and Zen in particular.

> Though Zen seems to me to be something that will appeal to an elite only, and a very small one, yet it has great importance because it is so closely related to such movements as phenomenology and existentialism, besides responding to certain inarticulate spiritual needs of man today. It is important that we know about it, and also I add that I think a little Zen discipline is a very healthy thing. However, there will also be a lot of irresponsible talk floating around, and this too must be taken into account. But it will pass. Let us hope the true substance remains, even though from the Zen point of view there isn't any substance anyway. (5.29.64 HGL 440)

By the fall of 1964, Thomas Merton had begun to contemplate a trip to Japan in order to experience Zen firsthand. He had judged that merely studying this contemplative tradition would not suffice, and in September he wrote of this to the German Jesuit scholar of Oriental thought Heinrich Dumoulin:

> The idea of going to Japan is not something that I had ever seriously dreamed of, but I had long been perfectly aware that I could not hope to make sense writing about Zen if I did not know the Zen life as it is lived in Japan, and did not know some Japanese. Hence it is clear that your suggestion is very timely and practical, and it seems to me to be perfectly in accord with the Spirit now sweeping through the Church, especially when there is much genuine concern about relationship with non-Christian religions. The mutual understanding of East and West also presents itself as one of the great spiritual tasks of our time. . . .
> . . . I would regard it as an immense grace to be able to come to Japan and meet you and your colleagues who are engaged

in this most important work, in order to get a firsthand acquaintance with Zen and be able to be more of a contemplative myself. (9.24.64 HGL 171–73)

By November, however, Merton realized such a trip would not be permitted by his abbot, Dom James Fox. Merton increased his awareness and understanding of the various strands of Buddhism and Zen practices. He wrote to Dumoulin about the differences between the school of Hui Neng and that of Shen Hsui. He was clearly moving toward an appreciation of the void at the center of consciousness, the "mind-without-concepts" that grasps what is most real.

> . . . words like "concentration" and "Konzentrationsübung" strike me as completely foreign to the Zen of Hui Neng. . . . When he declares that prajna and dhyana are the same, he seems to me to be saying also that the step from mind-with-concepts to mind-without-concepts is not a step which is taken, but that on the contrary Zen is the realization that the mind-with-concepts is empty and that the concepts themselves are emptiness. . . . it does seem to me to be the meaning of Hui Neng's verse, as opposed to that of Shen Hsui. (7.20.64 HGL 171)

At Easter of 1965 Merton wrote to Marco Pallis about his growing awareness of the inevitable differences between the great world religious traditions. One must always be firmly grounded in one's own tradition before one can enter and understand another one, he thought.

> . . . I agree entirely that one must cling to one tradition and to its orthodoxy, at the risk of not understanding any tradition. One cannot supplement his own tradition with little borrowings here and there from other traditions. On the other hand, if one is genuinely living his own tradition, he is capable of seeing where other traditions say and attain the same thing, and where they are different. The differences must be respected, not brushed aside, even and especially where they are irreconcilable with one's own view. (HGL 469)

Several months later, Merton seemed resigned both to the essential importance of interreligious dialogue for him as well as to the regrettable lack of understanding of this by others. As he wrote to Pallis:

> . . . I do think that you [are] representative of the ancient traditions, and I consider myself one of you, have a most important vocation in the world today. But we will not really be attended to. It does not much matter. I think that, for ourselves, we must consider at once a deeper penetration into and fidelity to the great wisdom of our fathers, *all* our fathers, with a deeper and deeper awareness of our unique responsibility to the wisdom of all the ancients, including the hidden and prehistoric ones. And at the same time be aware of our limitations, and the unlimited capacity of the power of the Spirit in us nevertheless, in the darkness and diaspora in which we live. I doubt if we are called upon to accomplish anything, but we will be what *we cannot help being*. This is the great truth that at once humbles and encourages us. On the basis of this awareness, I think there is every reason for a great boldness and freedom, but in a kind of Taoist dimension of not-striving. I am struck above all by the limitless depths of despair that are really implicit in the pitiful "hopes" of so many moderns, Christians, who are trying to come out with justifications for a completely secularized and optimistic eschatology of pseudo-science, in which the eventual triumph of religion is to discover that God is "dead" and that there is no religion anyway. The thing that we have seen is that this discovery is so old and so childish that it has been absorbed and explained millennia ago in the apophatic tradition, which results in the most positive of all the answers and affirmations, in apparent negation . . . (6.17.65 HGL 470–71)

During 1966 Merton was in communication with the Vietnamese Buddhist monk Thich Nhat Hanh, who had visited the Abbey of Gethsemani. Of him Merton wrote: "We had a Buddhist monk from Vietnam here, a very fine person, one of the leading Buddhist intellectuals there, a Buddhist existentialist and Zen monk. Thich Nhat Hanh is his name. I was very impressed with him. Pray for him" (Sr. M. Emmanuel, 6.13.66

HGL 197). In this exchange with the Buddhist monk Merton was finding even more commonality with Buddhists in the problems that both their spiritual systems and structures faced in relating to the world of the twentieth century.

> I think you make very clear what Buddhism really is. And I certainly feel very strongly as you do that the essential thing is to escape ignorance and the inevitable suffering that follows from it by a real contact with things as they are, instead of an illusory relationship with the world. I think your problems with conservative and formalist religiosity are very much the same as ours in the Catholic Church. It is the same everywhere. A new mentality is needed, and this implies above all a recovery of ancient and original wisdom. And a real contact with what is right before our noses. (6.29.66 HGL 382)

By early 1965 Thomas Merton's writings about Zen seemed to be more and more based on his own interior experience. Gone is talk of Buddhism being somewhat atheistic. Gone is the distinction between natural and supernatural. For Merton, then, Spirit is precisely what is within us, which is beyond a subject-object relationship. It is love-within. He wrote of this to William Johnston:

> It is quite true that in Zen there is little or nothing said about love . . . Still, apart from the completely a-personal theodicy, if you can call it that, I wonder if there is not all the same some love buried deep in Zen. Perhaps I am only projecting my own Christian experience into the Zen framework. It is sadly true that I have no real knowledge of Zen as it actually is in Japan. (1.25.65 HGL 441)

Later that year he wrote to Linda Sabbath:

> . . . the genuine Zen experience implies so much of humility, of selflessness, of self-emptying and renunciation, and the "void" seems to me to be so capable of being a masked fullness which might well be that of the Spirit . . . All these things make me think that some of the great Zen masters were certainly very

holy men and perhaps mystics in a certain sense. (The Zen people often reject the term "mystic," because to them it still implies a subject-object relationship with God. I think that is not so.) . . . (10.4.65 HGL 520)

In July of 1967, The Trappist again reflected with Johnston about the differences between Christian theism and Buddhism's unwillingness to discuss a "God" at all. He was becoming aware of what he spoke of as "a deep underlying connection of opposites" between theistic language and Buddhism's apparent atheism or agnosticism. Merton is very helpful here in helping Christians then and now to become aware of the spiritual experience that lies beyond, behind, and also within doctrinal concepts and verbal expressions. It is the Buddhist experience called "satori." He also indicates a typical attitude of indifference to methods and techniques for meditation and prayer.

> Honestly I do not think it matters a bit whether one can sit cross-legged or not. . . . Much more deep and difficult is the question of satori. . . .
> . . . the Japanese Zen people have their own rather schematic idea of what it means to "believe in God." Obviously, if it implies essentially a sort of subject-object relationship, then it means a "dualism" which categorically excludes satori. They probably have never investigated the witness of mystics like Eckhart for whom it is possible to be "so poor" that one does not even "have a God." This does not mean "Christian atheism" or "God-is-dead theology." It is simply a fact of a certain area of apophatic experience. Also the Japanese Zen people probably think of Christian mysticism in terms of "bridal mysticism," the gift of mystical rings, embraces, ecstasies and all that. Well, OK, no satori along those lines. . . .
> . . . for there to be a real satori the idea of "a Christian who can attain satori" has to go out the window as utterly irrelevant. . . .
> Personally I do not think satori is impossible for a Christian any more than it is for a Buddhist. In either case, one goes in a certain sense beyond all categories, religious or otherwise. But

perhaps our very attitude toward Christianity makes this harder for us. I do think it is probably best to simply take what Zen can offer us in the way of inner purification and freedom from systems and concepts, and not worry too much about precisely where we get. (7.5.67 HGL 442)

Thomas Merton's final comments on Buddhism in his published letters date from March 1968. While admitting a deepening appreciation for the thought of Shen Hui, perhaps over Hui Neng, the monk was beginning to find an even greater interest once again in Chinese religious literature: "The more I consider Shen Hui the more I see his importance and the more I like his Ch'an. Much as I find Zen appealing, I think the early masters of Ch'an are the best" (Richard S. Y. Chi, 3.14.68 HGL 124). Earlier the monk had written to Sufi Abdul Aziz of his deepening appreciation of this Chinese wisdom: "I find in Taoism something of the same spirit that is so central to all the other mystical movements everywhere" (1.30.61 HGL 46–47).

It was in writing the book on Chuang Tzu that the Trappist took his greatest delight. John Wu, the Chinese scholar and diplomat, had urged Merton to try his hand at this Chinese sage. Merton wrote to Wu's friend Paul Sih about his work on Chuang Tzu in 1961:

> . . . although I was scared to even think of it, I did a couple of short passages the other day and found they came out all right. At least I thought they did, but probably I have no real way of knowing. Of course it is just a matter of putting together three or four translations and then following hunches, which is what John [Wu] advised me to do, saying he would go over the finished product and make all the corrections. But it is hardly a work of scholarship, and honestly if this is going to be the procedure, I wonder if there is any point in your publishing the book. (5.23.61 HGL 549)

But by 1965 Merton was able to write with more confidence about this same work to Etta Gullick: "Chuang Tzu seems to have been on the right track in many respects, though without the theological depth that would come with true faith: still, he grasped the nature of things and of our orientation to God in silence" (6.9.65 HGL 370).

Later that year the Trappist wrote to Linda Sabbath about the Chuang Tzu book: "That book is what I mean, these days" (12.17.65 HGL 522). And even in 1968, in a letter to Christopher Mwoleka, Merton was still praising the outlook of this Chinese wise man in his connections with natural realities: "Chuang Tzu is very *open* to living things and relatively closed to artificial and social standards. I believe that one of the most beautiful things about African traditions would possibly be the sense of fellowship and brotherhood with other living beings, the animals etc., and with nature in general" (2.24.68 HGL 463).

In addition to Buddhism and Chinese writings, Thomas Merton's letters during the 1960s indicate a great interest in the Islamic Sufi tradition. He admits, however, to a somewhat limited knowledge of the Muslim tradition. It was the Sufi mystical dimension that appealed to him most, as he wrote to Abdul Aziz in January 1961: "Some of us in the community, and I am one of these, have aspirations for a more solitary and meditative form of prayer life. . . . I feel that in some respects our situation is a little analogous to that of the Sufis in their relation with the orthodox Moslem community with its emphasis on legal observance" (1.30.61 HGL 47).

In the previous year the monk had confessed to Aziz some of his earlier immature, critical comments about Sufism in a 1949 work of his. "As to *Seeds of Contemplation*, the reason why I have not added this to the others is, frankly, shame. The book was written when I was much younger and contains many foolish statements, but one of the most foolish reflects an altogether stupid ignorance of Sufism" (11.17.60 HGL 44).

One of Thomas Merton's principal contacts on Islam and the Sufi tradition was the renowned Islamic scholar Louis Massignon. Merton wrote about him in 1961 in a letter to Dona Luisa Coomaraswamy, the wife of Hindu and Buddhist scholar Ananda Coomaraswamy:

Massignon is one of the few Christians I know who has really deep and warm contacts with Moslems. Through him I have met one very ardent soul in Pakistan [Abdul Aziz]. You are right about the Sufis and about the need for Christian equivalents of the Sufis. . . . Men do not choose to be Sufis, least of all Christian Sufis so to speak: they are chosen and plunged into the crucible like iron into the fire. I do not know if I have been so chosen but I am familiar enough with the crucible, and I live under the sign of contradiction. Would that I might so live gently, non-violently, firmly, in all humility and meekness, but not betraying the truth.

But there is certainly a great need of an interior revival of truth, religious truth. (2.12.61 HGL 128)

Later that year the Trappist wrote about his deepening appreciation of Islam in a letter to Abdul Aziz, one of Merton's most frequent and most profound correspondents during the last decade of his life. He was particularly appreciative of the Islamic emphasis on the Oneness of the divinity that, he judged, did not necessarily compromise Christian belief in the Trinity.

I am tremendously impressed with the solidity and intellectual sureness of Sufism. There is no question but that here is a living and convincing truth, a deep mystical experience of the mystery of God our Creator Who watches over us at every moment with infinite love and mercy. I am stirred to the depths of my heart by the intensity of Moslem piety toward His Names, and the reverence with which He is invoked as the "Compassionate and the Merciful."

. . . The question of Tawhid is of course central and I think that the closest to Islam among the Christian mystics on this point are the Rhenish and Flemish mystics of the fourteenth century, including Meister Eckhart, who was greatly influenced by Avicenna. The culmination of their mysticism is in the "Godhead" beyond "God" (a distinction which caused trouble to many theologians in the Middle Ages and is not accepted without qualifications) but at any rate it is an ascent to perfect and ultimate unity beyond the triad in unity of Persons. This is a subtle and difficult theology and I don't venture into it without necessity . . . (5.13.61 HGL 48–49)

One year later, in writing to Aziz, Merton was finding that ". . . there is much in common, on the level of experience, between Sufism and Christian mysticism . . ." (4.4.62 HGL 51). The following year, 1963, Merton told Aziz that he was finding a kind of soul mate in the great Sufi writer Shaikh Ahmad. Of him Merton wrote: ". . . with someone like Shaikh Ahmad, I speak the same language and indeed have a great deal more in common than I do with the majority of my contemporaries in this country. In listening to him I seem to be hearing a familiar voice from my 'own country' so to speak" (10.18.63 HGL 55). Another Sufi mystic who impressed Merton was Ahmad Al-'Alawi, as he told English scholar Martin Lings in 1965: "He was so perfectly right in his spirituality. Certainly a great saint and a man full of the Holy Spirit" (4.24.65 HGL 454).

Merton continued his reflections to Aziz on the theological ways in which the Muslim emphasis on the oneness of God and the Christian emphasis on the three Persons in One God could, perhaps, be understood without inherent contradiction. Yet the Christian doctrine of incarnation would continue to be a stumbling block in agreement upon God's ways with the world.

> The chief thing that is to be stressed before all else is the transcendent UNITY of God. Now as this unity is beyond all number, it is a unity in which "one" and "three" are not numerically different. Just as Allah remains "one" while being compassionate and merciful, and His compassion and mercy represent Him in different *relations* to the world, so the Father and Son and Holy Spirit are perfectly One, yet represent different relations.
> . . . there seems to be much in common between our idea of the working of God in and through Christ and your idea of God manifesting Himself to the world in and through the

Prophet. I must leave this to future consideration. The one tech-
nical difference of a doctrine of the incarnation is of course
enormous.

I perfectly agree that any man who in his heart sincerely
believes in God and acts according to his conscience, with all
rectitude, will certainly be saved and will come to the vision of
God. . . .

. . . Hesychasm is to me very interesting and I think you
will find it the point of contact between Christian mysticism
and the Sufis. (10.18.63 HGL 56–57)

In 1964 Thomas Merton had been asked to make contribu-
tions about Islamic mysticism to his Order's journal, *Collectanea
Cisterciana*. He saw this as "a new step, and a promising one."
In his study of these ancient traditions of the East, Merton had
clearly begun to understand God's ways with others beyond
Christian revelation. As he wrote to Aziz: ". . . it should be
perfectly clear that Christian doctrine on this point is in accord
with common sense and the ordinary religious feeling of all
believers: obviously the ultimate destiny of each individual
person is a matter of his personal response to the truth and to
the manifestation of God's will to him, and not merely a matter
of belonging to this or that organization" (6.28.64 HGL 58).

Merton wrote in April of 1965 to Linda Sabbath that he was
". . . very much interested in contemplative disciplines of
other than Christian traditions, especially Zen and Sufism"
(4.25.65 HGL 517). However, he confessed to Martin Lings two
months later: "I am really quite lost in the field of Islamic studies, since obviously I have only the most superficial acquaintance with the field . . ." (6.20.65 HGL 454).

Merton began to compare and contrast the writings of the
Christian mystical tradition with writings of Sufis. He sensed
that St. John of the Cross had been ". . . influenced to some
extent by a Moroccan Sufi, Ibn Abbad" (Reza Arasteh, 12.18.65
HGL 41). And he judged that the principles of abandonment
of eighteenth-century French spiritual writer Jean Pierre de
Caussade were quite ". . . close in many ways to the ascesis
of Sufism" (Aziz, 1.16.68 HGL 66).

During the last year of Thomas Merton's life, he reported that he had been giving talks to the Gethsemani community on Sufi spirituality "for over a year." He based his thoughts on works being sent to him by Aziz such as one he considered to be among the best on the subject by Seyyed Hossein Nasr (4.24.68 HGL 66–67). During these spring months Merton had shared an article with Iranian psychologist Reza Arasteh entitled "Rebirth and the New Man in Christianity." He claimed that the article might provide Arasteh with ". . . some introduction to the idea of rebirth which is so important in Christianity—just as it is in Sufism" (3.22.68 HGL 42).

Thomas Merton's study of Hinduism was not extensive. He wrote in 1967 to Indian scholar and poet Amiya Chakravarty: ". . . I am bent on continuing to read about Hindu thought and deepening my appreciation of it" (1.10.67 HGL 113). Gandhi in particular was a Hindu person of interest and admiration for Merton. As he wrote to social activist James Douglass: "There is no question that Gandhi is in the end non-modern. His whole basis is in the Indian tradition and metaphysics. Like Camus, he is essentially a 'conservative,' in the sense of consciously keeping alive the continuity with a past wisdom stated in contemporary terms" (3.24.67 HGL 164).

One extensive commentary reflecting the Trappist's thoughts on the Indian religion was written in 1965, in a letter to a member of the Rama Krishna community in California named Philip Griggs. Merton reflected at some length on the relative merits of the different traditions in bringing one close to God.

> You ask about the relative nearness to God of a fervent Sadhu and a superficial Christian. The Church's teaching on nearness to God is that he who loves God better, knows Him better, and is more perfectly obedient to His will, is closer to Him than others who may love, know and obey Him less well. Since it is to me perfectly obvious that a Sadhu might well know God better and love Him better than a lukewarm Christian, I see no problem whatever about declaring that such a one is closer to Him and is even, by that fact, closer to Christ. The distinction lies in the fact that Catholics believe that the Church does

possess a clearer and more perfect exoteric doctrine and sacramental system which "objectively" ought to be more secure and reliable a means for men to come to God and save their souls. Obviously this cannot be argued and scientifically proved, I simply state it as part of our belief in the Church. But the fact remains that God is not bound to confine His gifts to the framework of these external means, and in the end we are sanctified not merely by the instrumentality of doctrines and sacraments but by the Holy Spirit. And I repeat my conviction as a Catholic that the Holy Spirit may perfectly well be more active in the heart of a Hindu monk than in my own. I am prepared to recognize this in anyone I meet who seems to be genuinely holy and I am quite often struck by what seem to me to be signs of such holiness in people who have nothing to do with the Catholic Church. On the other hand, I would not be so naive as to go around measuring the holiness of Hindu monks by this subjective standard . . . (6.22.65 HGL 338–39)

Then Merton comments theologically on nature and person in the Advaita and in the Christian understanding of the divinity. As always his thought seeks that "underlying connection of opposites." The Spirit is the same throughout for him.

[On Hindu saints:] . . . these holy men have received the gift of God, the Holy Spirit, and have become "divine" not by nature but "by adoption," not by creation but in the Spirit and in love. I state this, you understand, merely as an exposition of what all Catholics must hold, not as an attempted "refutation" of Advaita. What is important at this point is to do the groundwork of clarification on the concepts of *nature* and *person* and the corresponding concepts in Vedanta. I for one might question whether the Vedantic position is really conveyed in its fullness by treating *Atman* as a concept of *Nature*. And as corollary to that I would like for my own part to strongly repudiate confusion between the idea of person with the idea of *individual nature*. In Christian metaphysics I think it will be seen eventually that the idea of person far transcends that of nature, and this applies also to Christian theology. But I readily admit that most philosophy and theology has not yet made this clear . . . (6.22.65 HGL 339–40)

Thomas Merton's last contribution to interreligious dialogue was made during his final journey in life to Bangkok, Thailand, in late 1968. Throughout that year, ever since the election of Flavian Burns as his new abbot, he had been hoping to travel more in order to experience firsthand some of the great religious traditions of the East. As he wrote in March to Amiya Chakravarty: "I have been invited to a meeting of (Christian) monastic Superiors in Bangkok in December—but doubt if Thailand will be at peace in December. Meanwhile I am having a hard time getting this unusual permission to travel. My Abbot doubts that one of his monks ought to go so far—he is a new and young Abbot" (3.6.68 HGL 119).

By June he is somewhat more hopeful of at least some travels to the East. Again to Chakravarty:

> Though it is not certain that I shall attend the meeting at Bangkok I have received permission to go and preach a retreat at our Cistercian monastery in Indonesia. This will give me also an opportunity to visit some non-Christian monasteries in SE Asia and in Japan. . . . It is good to think that even if I don't get to the Bangkok meeting (to which I do not attach excessive importance) I may yet see the things I ought to see and meet some of the people I ought to meet. (6.14.68 HGL 120)

By July, Thomas Merton's final journey with destiny was in place as he wrote to Dorothy Day: "I have a big thing coming up. I am to go to Asia as peritus for a regional meeting of abbots and also to attend a meeting of leaders from non-Christian religions. I hope this may mean a deepening of understanding and a chance to enter more deeply into the mind of some of the Asian monastic traditions. Prayer will be the most vital help" (7.25.68 HGL 154).

Interreligious dialogue has progressed during the decades since Merton's death in Bangkok, Thailand, where he was addressing a conference on East and West monasticism. Yet the philosophical and theological implications of his thoughts and writings continue to intrigue both scholars and persons of a spiritual nature. The developments in this area push the envelope for the future of religion in the twenty-first century. As Hans Küng said: "There will be no peace among the nations without peace among religions. There will be no peace among the religions without dialogue among the religions" (March 2005, "Exhibit on the World's Religions," Santa Clara University). Thomas Merton, as in so many other areas, was a formidable forerunner in building bridges between Eastern and Western religious traditions.

9

On Monastic Renewal

From the day he entered the Abbey of Gethsemani on December 10, 1941, until his death on December 10, 1968, Fr. Louis Merton, OCSO, expended a great deal of time and energy studying the roots of monastic life. Based upon the best of the ancient monastic traditions, Merton developed his own thoughts over the years on the development and reform of monastic existence. He frequently wrote of his ever-changing ideas to his many correspondents around the world.

In 1954 he wrote to Erich Fromm about what he considered to be a mature ideal of monastic living. Here one can note the Trappist's early idealistic emphasis on the monks' withdrawal from the world. There is no expression at this time of his later concern for the existential failures in the practice of the coenobitic life.

> . . . the mature monk is a very capable and many-sided person, completely integrated, leading a life of freedom and joy under the guidance of the Holy Spirit rather than out of servile fear. In fact, servility is the exact opposite of the Christian and monastic spirit.
>
> . . . in the monastic life I think we are quite entitled to "escape" from certain responsibilities—those of worrying about how to plan meals, what to wear, when to get up, when to go

to bed, how to plan our social life, etc.—in order to be free for something better. (10.2.54 HGL 310)

On March 18, 1958, Thomas Merton became profoundly aware that his idealistic withdrawal from the world had gradually shifted. In Louisville, at the corner of Fourth and Walnut Streets, he had his now-famous moment of conversion back toward the world. He realized that he was in the monastery not just for his own salvation but also for others. Solitude had made him feel connected with others at ever-deeper levels. Rather than separating him from others, his monastic solitude and silence had led toward a deeper sense of union and communion with them.

As he watched other human beings moving around him on the busy street that day, the Trappist realized that he was not so different from ordinary persons at all. He was one of them and he loved them.

> Yesterday, in Louisville, at the corner of 4th and Walnut, suddenly realized that I loved all the people and that none of them were, or could be, totally alien to me. As if waking from a dream—the dream of my separateness, of my "special" vocation to be different. My vocation does not really make me different from the rest of men or just one in a special category, except artificially, juridically. I am still a member of the human race—and what more glorious destiny is there for man, since the Word was made flesh and became, too, a member of the Human Race! (Michael Mott, *The Seven Mountains of Thomas Merton*, 311)

From that experience onward, Fr. Louis expressed ever more clearly this connection between the monk and the world in his prayer and in his writings. For example, in November 1958, he wrote of his deepened awareness of this vital and profound connection to the world in a letter to the newly elected Pope John XXIII.

I hope that I can bring joy to the paternal heart of Your Holiness by sharing with you the aspirations of a contemplative monk who has always loved his vocation, especially the opportunity it offers for solitude and contemplation. . . . I have come to see more and more what abundant apostolic opportunities the contemplative life offers, without even going outside the monastic cloister.

It seems to me that, as a contemplative, I do not need to lock myself into solitude and lose all contact with the rest of the world; rather this poor world has a right to a place in my solitude. It is not enough for me to think of the apostolic value of prayer and penance; I also have to think in terms of a contemplative grasp of the political, intellectual, artistic and social movements in this world—by which I mean a sympathy for the honest aspirations of so many intellectuals everywhere in the world and the terrible problems they have to face. . . .

Most Holy Father, with the encouragement of friends and a number of priests and bishops, I am beginning to think seriously of the possibility of a monastic foundation, whose purpose would be to exercise a contemplative apostolate of this kind. . . .

. . . I want to ask, on my behalf and theirs, *if Your Holiness believes that there is a place for a limited apostolate of this kind . . .* in an Order that is strictly contemplative. And *if Your Holiness believes that special houses of this kind should exist,* with a staff that is more or less trained for this kind of apostolate. (11.10.58 HGL 482–83)

Four years later Monk Merton had become, even from his monastic setting, very reconnected with the world that he thought he had abandoned in 1941. From his monastic vantage point of contemplation, he wrote critically—but with compassion—of what he was hearing and seeing of certain social injustices in the world. For this the Trappist was at times severely criticized by some of his superiors and also those outside the monastery, including some prominent church leaders. They thought that monks were in no position to know about such worldly affairs and should stick to their prayers.

Some of Merton's writings on these matters were extensively censored by his own Trappist Order both in the United States and in Rome. Merton found this frustrating and, at times, pointless. He judged his own monastic vocation as a prophet to be thwarted by such exercises of official blindness. He expressed his strong feelings with passionate cynicism and irony to the young social activist James Forest in 1962.

> . . . The monk is the one supposedly attuned to the inner spiritual dimension of things. If he hears nothing, and says nothing, then the renewal [of the Church] as a whole will be in danger and may be completely sterilized. But these authoritarian minds believe that the function of the monk is not to see or hear any new dimension, simply to support the already existing viewpoints precisely insofar as and because they are defined for him by somebody else . . . The function of the monk . . . then becomes simply to affirm his total support of officialdom. He has no other function, then, except perhaps to pray for what he is told to pray for: namely the purposes and objectives of an ecclesiastical bureaucracy. The monastery as dynamo concept goes back to this. The monk is there to generate spiritual power that will justify over and over again the already predecided rightness of the officials above him. He must in no event and under no circumstances assume a role that implies any form of spontaneity and originality. He must be an eye that sees nothing except what is carefully selected for him to see. An ear that hears nothing except what it is advantageous for the managers for him to hear. We know what Christ said about such ears and eyes. (4.29.62 HGL 267)

Twice during 1963 Thomas Merton wrote vividly of his sense of the relations between the monastery and the world. To Jesuit Dan Berrigan, on the one hand, he reported his disgust with the failure of monastic leaders to be realistic about the world: "And now about the monastic life and ideal, in relation to the world. Look, I hate to be vulgar, but a lot of the monastic party line we are getting, even where in some respects it is very good, ends up by being pure unadulterated——crap" (6.25.63 HGL 78).

On the other hand, to British layman Marco Pallis, who was interested in Tibetan monasticism, Merton pointed out the antithetical nature of the monastic and the American cultures: "Though there is now such a thing as an "American" monasticism, which is in its way fairly genuine, we must remember that this country lives by everything that is hostile to a truly monastic life, and even its most cordial embraces tend to prove deadly in the long run" (July 1963 HGL 464).

During the 1960s Thomas Merton wrote two letters to the Bishop of Rome about monastic life. In 1964 he wrote to Pope Paul VI in the midst of Vatican II about the renewal of the church and monasticism. Monastic culture has a very unique and distinct contribution to make, according to the Trappist.

> We dare to believe that the monastic life may have a very special role in the renewal of the Church. There is much that is paradoxical in monasticism, and this paradox tends to be lost sight of when the monastic Orders are treated just like other religious Orders. In effect, the monk can do most for the world when he is most truly solitary. Yet even in his solitariness he must retain some physical contact with "the world." Does it seem that the somewhat charismatic character of this monastic apostolate might be more appreciated? Then the effect of the monk's life of prayer and his ability to share with others the fruits of contemplation would not be obscured or submerged in the routines and pressures of a more organized apostolate. In a word, we monks wish to assure Your Holiness of our deep sense of our need for a monastic renewal in deeper poverty, simplicity, solitude and prayer, which will at the same time give meaning to those contacts which we do and should have with intellectuals (Christian and otherwise) and with those interested in ecumenism, as well as with the ordinary faithful. (2.6.64 HGL 488)

Writing to the pope again in 1967, Merton discussed the necessary and fruitful tension between the interior and exterior dimensions of religious life. Based upon his own experiences at Gethsemani, he proposed ways in which monks could remain contemplative yet also make a contribution to the active

life of the church. No doubt he had himself in mind as one
ready and willing to move beyond the cloister with a message
of the contemplative mind and heart.

> It would seem that the main question of renewal in the monastic
> Orders centers around the truly contemplative and interior life.
> I think most of us realize this, but there is a division of opinions
> between those who think that the interior life will be renewed if
> external protection is guaranteed (strict enclosure, etc.). Others
> see the importance of a deep interior renewal to be attained by
> a return to the ancient sources in spirit, while keeping in mind
> the mentality and special needs of modern man. It appears to
> me that both views have to be considered: silence and enclosure
> should be indeed maintained, but at the same time there must
> be new elements of openness and dialogue, better instruction
> and greater freedom for monks to participate in conferences
> and other useful meetings. In my own experience I realize the
> fruitfulness and importance of dialogue with visitors who come
> to the monastery and who belong to non-Catholic or even non-
> Christian traditions of spirituality.
>
> In the light of this I ask myself if there might not be special
> possibilities of a monastic apostolate which would be primarily
> contemplative and which would consist not only in providing
> a place of prayer and retreat, with a certain amount of instruc-
> tion and direction, but also Christian contemplatives could
> engage in well-informed and prudent dialogue with specialists
> in the field of non-Christian religions, particularly contempla-
> tive forms of non-Christian monasticism.
>
> As to the problem of contemplatives engaging in the ordi-
> nary apostolate—a problem which excites fear in some mem-
> bers of our Order—a possible solution might be this: that the
> Order as such would maintain its strict contemplative character,
> but that individual members of it who might feel called to offer
> themselves for active work, for instance in a mission field, for
> several years, should not be prohibited or discouraged, but
> should be encouraged to do so, with the possibility of returning
> to their monasteries after a few years of active work. It is pos-
> sible that their own religious vocations might benefit from this
> experience. (10.11.67 HGL 491)

Merton's thoughts about contemplation in action had been developing throughout his monastic life. As he wrote about the renewal of monastic witness, he was constantly criticizing both excessive withdrawal from the world on the one hand, and on the other, overly active monastic practices. To his Brazilian friend Sr. M. Emmanuel de Souza e Silva, he expressed in May of 1964 some of this tensive balance that must be strived for in any true and more simple monastic living.

> I was much criticized by some in the Order about "Monk in the Diaspora," for seeming to question the solidity of our façade in full view of the public. Actually I think most of our problems here are in the mind, and in the way we insist on thinking about ourselves. The situation could be a lot worse, and we could certainly make use of what we have in order to enter deeply into the mystery of the monastic life. Instead we are so insecure that we get involved (a) in useless activity, (b) in useless projects and revolutions, (c) in useless theorizing about our state and (d) in useless self-justification. . . . But it worked out all right. I think that if all goes well, we will normally and naturally simplify our own life. On the other hand, there are all those projects . . . What we want is not Trappists working in factories but Trappists who are monks, and real monks, not just sustainers of a monastic edifice which is very impressive to the world and very "regular" and well organized within. (5.31.64 HGL 190)

In November of 1964 the Trappist expressed some of his fears about a monasticism too organized around external observances, necessary as those may be for stable monastic life. Such a life does favor contemplative prayer and living, he said in a letter to Catherine de Hueck Doherty.

> The monasteries both of common life and of hermits . . . are organized in a rigid and stereotyped way for one kind of life only, which is not bad in its own way, and which seems to persist because it is relatively easy to keep in order. It is a matter of rules and observances which keep the monk busy and enable

him to live a life of comparative recollection and prayer, protecting him against some of the distractions of life, keeping him in trim by a certain amount of austerity.

Unfortunately this regimented form of existence, which is sound enough when based on the best traditions, tends to be rather empty and frustrating, to many vocations, and indeed there is a very general feeling that the life easily becomes a dead end. It retains its meaning for those who have some kind of responsibility in the community or who work in a way that contributes to the community, while for others, well, they tend to vegetate. There are few real contemplatives who can continue simply to live the monastic life as it is organized and really *grow* as they go on. . . .

There is also a very keen sense of need for a simpler, more "open" type of monastic life, in which the work will be more "real" and there will be more sense that one is living as ordinary poor people live, not as institutionalized and dressed-up "poor monks" with personal poverty in a rich community. (11.21.64 HGL 21)

During 1965 Thomas Merton wrote at least three times of his concerns for the renewal of monastic life, once to a layman and twice to a woman religious. In June he commented to the Russian Orthodox scholar Sergius Bolshakoff about some monastic experiments, in which monks were becoming more "relevant" through assuming positions in worldly occupations. As Fr. Louis neared his time for entering into his hermitage at Gethsemani, he was more convinced than ever that monks must be truly monks.

. . . I am in perfect agreement with your hesitations in approving the new trends on the part of some monks toward activism. I readily grant that the motives are good, and that the desire to help the Church is most laudable. But it seems to me that whatever may be the value of the means chosen, they are foreign to monasticism. . . . what I have heard about the experiments in trying to combine a contemplative life on the Trappist pattern with factory work strikes me as completely inauthentic and

ambiguous. It is neither honest factory work nor serious contemplative solitude. It is simply naive and well-meant game
without too much relation to the realities of the age or the exigencies of the monastic vocation. It seems to me that if we want
to take our true place in our time then we must recognize that
our place is that of *monks*. And the more perfectly we try to live
in the monastic tradition of simplicity, solitude, prayer, silence,
etc., the better we will justify our existence in the world, though
there is no need for us even to think of "justifying ourselves."
God is our only justification . . . . (6.9.65 HGL 105)

In July of 1965, one month before moving from the coenobitic to the eremitical life at the Abbey of Gethsemani, Fr. Louis
wrote to Sr. M. Emmanuel about what he perceived to be confusion among monks and leaders of the Order regarding just
what monastic existence should be. He appeared to be moving
toward thinking of contemplative life as not so confined to
monastic ways, and seemed less concerned about the renewal
of the institution of monasticism.

I think that though things are quiet here now, our Order is in
for a lot of trouble. There are many articulate desires for change,
and there is much going on (certainly it was a great step that
the General Chapter formally acknowledged that hermits were
permissible in our Order). But on the other hand there is much
confusion and incomprehension, and personally I do not think
that the grave situation can be met even with some much
needed changes. The confusion of motives and ideas is still too
great and the monks for the most part are not stable enough or
mature enough (in the U.S. at least) to assimilate what is going
on and make good use of it. Basically, they do not know what
they want, but they are sincere in their seeking. . . .
   . . . After all what matters is not simply to be a monk or a
nun but to be a Christian and a perfect disciple, open in heart
and mind to God's word. The trash will be thrown out of our
lives, and God knows there is plenty of trash in them. But we
will absolutely not see any real peace and perfection in religious
life in the next ten or fifteen years. That need not prevent us

from being happier than we ever were. I am not concerned with the perfect realization of monastic ideals any more. I see that there is really nothing much I can do about it. The system is too big and too clumsy and too much of a system . . . (7.11.65 HGL 194–95)

The year 1967 found Thomas Merton discussing monastic renewal extensively with his many correspondents, and it was with a much different tone and agenda than was expressed in his 1954 letter to Erich Fromm, quoted at the beginning of this chapter. The Trappist had become quite critical of monastic renewal in general and of the Abbey of Gethsemani in particular. During that year Merton engaged in a long series of letters with the young theologian Rosemary Radford Ruether. Although critical of Gethsemani and monastic structures in general, Merton, from his hermitage, still judged that he was following his true vocation—even though it looked less and less monastic in externals.

About monasticism, my vocation and all that. . . . I always tend to assume that everyone knows I have had a monumental struggle with monasticism as it now is and still disagree violently with most of the party-line policies. I am a notorious maverick in the Order and my Abbot considers me a dangerous subject, always ready to run off with a woman or something, so I am under constant surveillance. If I am allowed to live in a hermitage it is theoretically because this will keep me more under wraps than otherwise. So when I say I "have no problem with my vocation," I just mean that I am not for the moment standing over the Abbot with a smoking gun in my hand. In other words I have the usual *agonia* with my vocation but now, after twenty-five years, I am in a position where I am practically laicized and de-institutionalized, and living like all the other old bats who live alone in the hills in this part of the country and I feel like a human being again. My hermit life is expressly a *lay* life. I never wear the habit except when at the monastery and I try to be as much on my own as I can and like the people around the country. Also I try as best I can to keep up valid and living contacts with my friends who are in the thick of things, and everyone knows where my real "community" is. I honestly believe that is the right place for me (woods, not Gethsemani) insofar as it is the right battleground. It is a sort of guerrilla-outpost type of thing if you like. But from my experience I would myself be leading a less honest and more faked life if I were back in the cities. This is no reflection on anyone else. In staying here I am not just being here for myself but for my friends, my Church, and all those I am one with. Also, if there is one thing I am sure of too, it is my need to fight out in my own heart whatever sort of fight for honesty I have to wage and for fidelity to God. I am not by any means turning my back on other people, I am as open as the situation (of overcontrol) permits and want to make this more open as time goes on. Lots of people would like me to get out and join them in this or that, but I just don't see that I could do it without getting into some absurd role and having to act a dumb part or justify some nonsense or other that I don't really believe in. I know I firmly disbelieve all the favorite clichés about monasticism, and the community knows it too. I can't say where and how my life is eschatological, because as far as I can see I am a tramp and not much else. But this kind of tramp is what I am supposed to be. This kind of place is where I am finally reduced to my nothingness and have to depend on God. Outside I would be much more able to depend on talk. Maybe I am just protesting too much, but that is the way I feel about it. I assure you that whatever else it is it is not complacency, because there is ample material for not being complacent, I assure you . . . (2.14.67 HGL 501–2)

Ruether replied immediately. She questioned the honesty of Merton's sense of his vocation. She upset him by calling into question his integrity and even his validity as a monk. In those activist years of the 1960s she was challenging the relevance of monasteries and the contemplative life. For her, monasticism seemed like an evasion of the serious Christian responsibility to change the world toward the kingdom of God. Merton responded by agreeing, yet also disagreeing, with Ruether.

Once this more existential view of the whole monastic situation becomes possible, then I think it is possible to agree with you that monasticism has "lost its soul" insofar as it has become committed to an ironbound institutionalism built on a perverse doctrine of authority-humility-obedience. The bind here is worse than anywhere else in the Church, insofar as the emphasis on perfect obedience as "the" monastic virtue (which of course it is not) puts the monk bound hand and foot in the power of his "prelate" (now no longer charismatic and chosen spiritual Father but his boss and feudal lord and maybe general in chief). Then when renunciation of the world is fitted into this context by being a prohibition of any sight or sound of anything outside the walls, and so on, plus a Jansenistic repudiation of all pleasure, then you do get a real monastic hell: I don't deny that at all, I have lived in one. But again, the answer is to start with saving the poor blighters that are caught in such a mess, and to save the beautiful life that has been turned into a hell for them, when it should be what it was first intended to be. (3.9.67 HGL 504–5)

At the same time that he was criticizing monastic life in general and at Gethsemani in particular, Fr. Louis was having some new dreams about gathering like-minded persons together to pursue deeper Christian values and ways of life. Reflecting perhaps his correspondence with Ruether in which she had described Church more as "a happening," the monk wrote to Daniel Berrigan: "I just got walloped with a terrific idea: a happening that could be possible down here. A get-together of extreme people to talk of community and particularly on the most radical level the prophetic and monastic type community and in what terms monasticism is even tolerable as a Christian concept any more" (3.7.67 HGL 93).

Thomas Merton had often dreamed of moving from Gethsemani to another place with more solitude and silence. At times he thought of establishing such a community himself along with others. As far back as 1958 he had written of these inner longings to Catherine de Hueck Doherty. He expressed a desire to:

. . . break off and start a new kind of small monastery in Ecuador, a sort of an ashram for local intellectuals and men of good will and Indians, part of the time devoted to discussions and spiritual works of mercy (and some corporal, like a clinic) and part of the time devoted to sitting in a hermitage and getting the straws out of my hair. The whole thing from a certain aspect looks more like Madonna House than O.C.S.O. . . . Anyway, there is no indication that it would possibly be the will of God, or at least not in the extreme form, and so I put it away as a temptation . . . (9.18.58 HGL 17)

The Cistercian Order, especially since its seventeenth-century reform by Abbot Armand Jean de Rance at the Abbey of Notre Dame de la Grande Trappe, had been noted for its austerity and extreme asceticism. This characterized life at the Abbey of Gethsemani at the time of Merton's arrival there in 1941. But during his twenty-seven years as a monk, the rigidities of the customs and the severe ascetical practices began to be considerably mitigated. During his final years the Kentucky Trappist shared with Rosemary Ruether his own thoughts about traditional asceticism. They reflect that of "the lay monk" and his developing sense of the monastic vocation as something quite human, humane, and natural. He was quite sharp in his exchange with her.

Honestly, your view of monasticism is to me so abstract and so in a way arbitrary (though plenty of basis in texts can be found) that it is simply poles apart from the existential, concrete, human dimension which the problem has for us here. . . . Let me put it this way: I am so far from being "an ascetic" that I am in many ways an antiascetic humanist, and one of the things in monasticism that has always meant most to me is that monastic life is in closer contact with God's good creation and is in many ways simpler, saner and more human than life in the supposedly comfortable, pleasurable world. One of the things I love about my life, and therefore one of the reasons why I would not change it for anything, is the fact that I live in the woods and according to a tempo of sun and moon and season in which it is naturally easy and possible to walk in God's light, so to speak, in and through his creation. That is why the narcissist bit in prayer and contemplation is no problem out here, because in fact I seldom have to fuss with any such thing as "recollecting myself" and all that rot. All you do is breathe, and look around. And wash dishes, type, etc. Or just listen to the birds. I say this in all frankness, realizing that I can be condemned for having it so much better than almost anybody. That is what I feel guilty about, I suppose, but certainly not that I have repudiated God's good creation. Sure, it is there in the cities too, but in such a strained, unnatural, tense shape . . . Absolutely the last thing in my own mind is the idea that the monk de-creates all that God has made. On the contrary, monks are, and I am, in my own mind, the remnant of desperate conservationists. . . . In a word, to my mind the monk is one of those who not only saves the world in the theological sense but saves it literally, protecting it against the destructiveness of the rampaging city of greed, war, etc. And this loving care for natural creatures becomes, in some sense, a warrant of his theological mission and ministry as a man of contemplation. . . .

. . . [This is] an example of what I myself am doing in my "secularized" existence as hermit. I am not only leading a more "worldly" life (me and the rabbits), but am subtly infecting the monastery with worldly ideas. I still am requested to give one talk a week in community, and have covered things like Marxism and the idea of dialogue à la Garaudy, Hromadka and so on, and especially all kinds of literary material, Rilke for some time, and now for a long time a series of lectures on Faulkner and his theological import. This is precisely what I think a hermit ought to do for the community which has seen fit deliberately and consciously to afford him liberty. I have a liberty which can fruitfully serve my brothers, and by extension I think it indicates what might be the monk's role for the rest of the Church . . . (3.9.67 HGL 502–5)

When the twenty-seven-year-old Thomas Merton arrived to join the Cistercian community at Gethsemani in 1941, he spoke of that place as the "center of America." It was what was holding the country together. As the doors closed behind him in the cloister, he spoke of having found "the four walls of my new freedom." By the 1960s Merton became much more realistic about his abbey. He had grown spiritually there sufficiently to the point of seeing its limitations and blind spots—its own humanness—as well as his own.

To Daniel Berrigan in June of 1962 he spoke of Gethsemani as a ". . . bigger and slower group" (6.29.62 HGL 74). In September of the same year he told Berrigan that he would find greater value in small groups and personal contacts than in the large monastery. "Things like the Little Brothers, and small ventures like Damasus Winzen's monastery strike me as being the real thing. Perhaps some of the aspects of what goes on at Gethsemani may have reality, but other aspects definitely not" (9.2.62 HGL 75).

One year later, the Trappist wrote to Dorothy Day of his commitment to remain at Gethsemani despite his frustrations with the place. Merton knew he was accepted at the monastery, or at least tolerated.

> . . . I am no stronger than anybody else, but it seems to me that I am almost bound to stay here even for the worst motives, let alone the best. Here is one place where they will have me and feed me and tolerate my presence permanently. How do I know I would find the same charity elsewhere? Tramp as I am, I think this is sufficient inducement, even if there were not the question of heaven to which I am not, I think, insensitive. . . . I am here and unless the Lord pulls me out by the hair of the head (and there is no hair left) I will probably remain here, as far as I know. I have no other plans. (9.5.63 HGL 147)

By 1965, in the spring before he was given permission to move into his hermitage near the monastery, Merton wrote of his Order as ". . . still very conservative in a stuffy sense, and slowly evolving to a more open position . . ." (Martin Lings, 4.24.65 HGL 453). And within a few months after having moved out of the large institution into the woods, he wrote to Canadian psychiatrist Raymond Prince of his insights about the potential and real narcissism of monastic living: "I notice, living as a hermit, that monastic community life permits a kind of communal narcissism which siphons it all off into community projects and a sort of communal awareness which is nevertheless centered in the self multiplied (rather than in real interpersonal love). In solitude one confronts narcissism in its brute form, and either resists or succumbs completely" (12.18.65 HGL 495).

By the spring of 1966, Hermit Merton felt sufficiently detached from the monastic institution and settled into the eremitical pattern of living that he could write to Marco Pallis: "As things are now going, it seems to me that without disrespect to my own community, being now more or less detached from it, I no longer profit much by its teachings and its programs, which in any case are taking a quite different direction from that which I myself am following" (5.28.66 HGL 476). Shortly thereafter Merton noted the noise of machinery down in the abbey, as the church was undergoing renovation. Such noise and machines and busyness always irritated Merton about Gethsemani—even from far away in the woods. "There is a great deal of noise in the monastery. The church and cloister are being renovated and I can hear the machines all the way out here at the hermitage. The new church will be simple and modern and I suppose it will be acceptable to most of the community" (Sr. M. Emmanuel, 6.13.66 HGL 196).

It is interesting to note that the Trappist's complaints about his abbey, as expressed in his published letters, were written to persons outside of monastic living. His greatest honesty may have been in his extensive correspondence with Rosemary Ruether during 1967.

> All this outcry about freedom.
> Refusal to grapple with the idea of monastic renewal because I see that too much is really involved, and that what is going on here now is superficial: what is really in question is the survival of the kind of thing we have here. They are trying to save it, or at least the general structure. I realize obscurely that

it can't be saved, has to be entirely rebuilt from the bottom up . . . (3.25.67 HGL 510)

Ruether responded, describing "the monastic-eschatological bit" as "one of mankind's magnificent illusions" (Mary Tardiff, ed., *At Home in the World*, 554). Merton seemed to agree to some extent, at least. He shared his dreams of joining a religious community in Chile—still restless after all of those years to find a more perfect monastic setting for himself. "Very good bit in your letter about my situation here. It is very unhealthy. I have thought about the various angles and still am. My present move is to try to get transferred to Chile. There the situation would be much better, at least. For the rest I still agree with you, but I'd need to talk about it more and see it clearer in this concrete case" (9.11.67 HGL 515).

The Trappist wrote in a similar vein a few days later to W. H. Ferry, in California:

> In a burst of something or other I tried to get myself transferred to Chile, to live as a hermit in the Andes and get out from under this goddamn overkill society. The permission was indignantly refused (was told to stay and save the society from within—i.e., to bust my skull against the impossible). Doesn't matter that much, really. Wherever one is, one is only an ambassador of affluence and napalm . . . (9.14.67 HGL 234)

And again, a few days later, he expressed himself to Dorothy Day with some self-deprecating humor:

> . . . Recently I offered to go to our foundation in Chile, largely because I thought it would be a way of renouncing my citizenship and becoming a citizen of a country that does not have the bomb and probably never will have it. My Abbot is inexorable on keeping me here where the image of Gethsemani won't suffer. It is odd to think that I am supposed to be an edification: I am glad people don't know me! I'd rather be a disedification, and do something worthwhile. Naturally, I am only joking. (9.19.67 HGL 153)

His final comments on his relationship to the Abbey of Geth-semani, found in the collected and published correspondence, came a few months before he departed for his Asian pilgrimage—from which he would not return. In this letter to the young Black tenor Robert Lawrence Williams, Merton was very down on that "center of America" that he had initially described as "the four walls of his new freedom." "As a Trappist, I can say I lived for twenty-five years in a situation in which I had NO human and civil rights whatever. Anything I got I had to beg for in an ignominious way. But I also had luck, as some do. I may be a success of sorts, but I can tell you what it amounts to: exactly zero" (7.16.68 HGL 605).

10

On the Church

Thomas Merton never developed any intentional or systematic ecclesiology in his extensive published writings. He did not represent any particular theological view of the church. In fact, his published writings tell little of what Merton thought about the church. Ecclesiology was not a matter of particular interest to this Trappist monk. Merton found his Catholicism in monastic life more than in the complex structures and laws of the institutional Roman Catholic Church. In a very real way, he found his "church" in his many and diverse friends and correspondents.

In his published correspondence, one can glean something of Merton's very personal reflections on the Roman Catholic Church. There he wrote of his experience of church as one of its monastic members in correspondence with others interested in the church. His correspondents include Roman Catholics, persons from various Christian denominations, some from other religions, and a few of no particular religious tradition at all. To one and all Merton writes always from the context of a Roman Catholic monk, both in agreement and dissent from institutional issues. And from these words about the church expressed chronologically in these many letters, we can learn something of the operative ecclesiology of Thomas Merton.

One sees in these uncensored writings Merton's developing thoughts about the church.

During the late 1930s Thomas Merton was doing graduate study at Columbia University in New York City. He was clearly searching for something more significant and satisfying in his life than he had found in his earlier years, wandering around France and England, and in his journeys with his father, painter Owen Merton. Tom Merton had grown up largely without church connections and without much religious information or formation. In his 1948 autobiography *The Seven Storey Mountain*, he wrote: ". . . for you must understand that while I admired Catholic *culture*, I had always been afraid of the Catholic Church" (188).

At Columbia, his friends Ed Rice, a Catholic, and Robert Lax, a Jew, along with two of his professors, Dan Walsh and Mark Van Doren, encouraged him to read serious religious literature. He read Etienne Gilson's *The Spirit of Medieval Philosophy* and Aldous Huxley's *Ends and Means*, which impressed Merton in that it "was preaching mysticism." From there his reading expanded to St. Augustine, Thomas à Kempis, and William Blake. In these intellectual and spiritual classics Tom Merton began to find spiritual light in his own human darkness. He relished the clarity and certitude of Catholicism, which he sensed might quell his intellectual uncertainties and personal uneasiness. This happened most profoundly for him in reading *Art and Scholasticism* by Jacques Maritain (*Seven Storey Mountain*, 217).

Merton began to attend Mass at Corpus Christi Church near the university, in Morningside Heights. In those Catholic rituals he felt a sense of awe and reverence that seemed to uplift the worshipers out of ordinariness into the realm of the sacred. This moved him deeply.

Merton was finding a far more sacred experience than he had felt in his few earlier contacts with Protestant churches. Before long he was taking instructions in the Catholic faith from Fr. Moore, an assistant pastor at Corpus Christi. He was bap-

tized there on November 16, 1938, with Ed Rice as his godfather.
After his first confession and first reception of Holy Communion that day, this seeker for truth was ecstatic. "For now
I had entered into the everlasting movement of that gravitation
which is the very life and spirit of God: God's own gravitation
towards the depths of His own infinite nature, His goodness
without end. And God, that center Who is everywhere, and
whose circumference is nowhere, finding me, through incor-
poration with Christ, incorporated into this immense and tremendous gravitational movement which is love, which is the
Holy Spirit, loved me" (*Seven Storey Mountain*, 246). Throughout his life the Mystical Body of Christ was an operative metaphor in Merton's own spirituality and ecclesiology.

Thomas Merton's conversion to Roman Catholicism was,
in many ways, an intellectual conversion. It seems to have been
stimulated more by his study of Catholicism than by any extensive experiences of the life of the Catholic Church. At that
time he did not appear to have any great questions or doubts
about the shape and style of Roman Catholicism as it was in
those days. The church of the Council of Trent and of Vatican
I seemed firmly in place and caused him no difficulty. For him
the solid and universal Roman Catholic Church, the Bark of
Peter, seemed like a kind of life raft to jump onto in order to
save himself from sinking in the turbulent sea of his personal
chaos and confusion.

He described his conversion to Catholicism to Rosemary
Radford Ruether in February of 1967: ". . . my coming into
the Church was marked by a pretty strong and dazzled belief
in the Christ of the Nicene Creed. One reason for this was a
strong reaction against the fogginess and subjectivity and
messed-up-ness of the ideas about Christ that I had met with
up and down in various types of Protestantism. I was tired of
a Christ who had evaporated" (Mary Tardiff, ed., *At Home in
the World*, 22).

Thomas Merton's initial enthusiasm and acceptance of
Roman Catholicism was tempered over the years in the light

of further study, and especially through his experiences of the church. In his mature years he modified his awareness of what church is and what it is not—what it claims to be in essence and what it existentially is. The monk discovered that Roman Catholic spiritual existence is not, in the long run, about the security that comes with having the right set of questions and answers. Life in the church is far riskier than that. The church as a "life raft" was simply a starting point for him. Once he felt safe enough in the arms of Mother Church and his monastic home at Gethsemani Abbey, he jumped back into the complexities of the flowing stream of real living and swam with the many new questions raised by his experience of church and world.

By 1959 Merton's understanding of church had been honed by the realities of its imperfections as well as its wonders. In March of that year he wrote of the church as a mixed bag of the good and the bad—like every person, including himself. He penned his thoughts to John Harris, an English layman who was having some difficulties with the church.

> There is and there can be nothing wrong with the Gospels and with Christianity. But often there are things and ideas that get mixed up with it, and seem even to be inseparable from it, or identified with it—and among these there are many errors, or wrong attitudes, or approaches to life that are not perfectly healthy. It is unfortunate that one has to run into these, and get mixed up in them to a certain extent. We cannot demand that our Christianity be absolutely pure . . . There is inevitably plenty of prejudice and cant wherever there is a religion. The point is that the wheat and the cockle are not the same thing, and that Christ Himself said, "Let both grow until the harvest." The temptation to demand that the wheatfield be absolutely pure cockle is then a real and serious temptation. It is really an evasion. We have to take on the difficult job of constantly making distinctions and telling the difference and adjusting ourselves to the reality, in order to make sure that we ourselves are wheat and not cockle. And of course the thing is that one never can tell. Because we are not the ones appointed to do the

judging. To look for an absolute assurance that one is pure wheat is to fall, after all, into the same old pharisaism. (3.14.59 HGL 387).

In April of the same year Fr. Louis wrote that the church as an institution could become a prisoner of its own formulas, laws, and structures. "As you know, the problem of writing down things about Christianity is fraught with ludicrous and overwhelming difficulties. No one cares for fresh, direct and sincere intuitions of the Living Truth. Everyone is preoccupied with formulas" (Daisetz T. Suzuki, 4.11.59 HGL 564). And in June the Trappist expressed concern over the church's excessive concern with externals: "The Church has made such a fuss over her externals, or rather Catholics have, that one coming in from the outside tends to worry about what is and is not 'done.' But in fact almost anything is 'done' in many cases, and it doesn't matter" (Harris, 6.22.59 HGL 391).

Merton's correspondent, John Harris, had introduced a case for the annulment of his marriage, which had reached the Roman courts. Harris had become frustrated with the slow handling of his marriage case in the Roman Curia and wrote to his monk-friend for encouragement and advice. Merton sympathized in words sharply critical of Roman bureaucratic practices: "I shall certainly pray that Rome gets galvanized into action and completes your [marriage] case. It is said that the Church itself is a permanent miracle witnessing to her own divine origin by her manifestly divine qualities. However, I think the machinery of the Roman Curia does not always bear this out, unless the eternity of God is conceived as a vacuum without activity in it" (9.7.60 HGL 397).

Thomas Merton's sense of the church as a reality deeper than its organizational structures and rules is evident in a letter to Abraham Heschel in 1960.

There are so many voices heard today asserting that one should "have religion" or "believe," but all they mean is that one should associate himself, "sign up" with some religious group.

> Stand up and be counted. As if religion were somehow primar-
> ily a matter of gregariousness. Alas, we have too much gregari-
> ousness of the wrong kind, and with results that do not need
> to be recalled. The gregariousness even of some believers is a
> huddling together *against* God rather than adoration of His true
> transcendent holiness. (12.17.60 HGL 431)

In early 1961, Merton used one of most beautiful metaphors
of the church: the Mother of Truth. This was in response to an
article on church unity written by Archimandrite Sophrony,
an Orthodox priest living in a monastic community in England.
Yet even here, the Trappist indicated his awareness that truth
cannot be equated with ecclesiastical formulas or rules. Truth
cannot be limited to any single theological school of thought.
One must be open to all truth, whatever its source. Truth must
be lived in every Christian life—including his own. His words
indicate the direction his life was already taking toward interreligious study, prayer, and dialogue. He was searching in
truth for what he later termed "the underlying connections of
opposites."

> . . . I enjoyed your article on the Unity of the Church. . . .
> Above all, I try to live out the consequence of that doctrine,
> namely, to unite in myself all Christian truth and all Christian
> love so that every Christian, and indeed everyone who is au-
> thentically in Christ, might take flesh in my life, or at least in
> my love. We must love the truth wherever it is found; we must
> go straight to the truth without wanting to glance backward
> and without caring about what school of theology it represents.
> The Church must truly be our Mother, which means that she
> must be the Church of the love of Christ; she must welcome us
> with a mother's love that shares her wisdom with us. You surely
> know the distress that one must experience in seeking to find
> the truth of love instead of the truth of formulas . . . and of
> laws, of programs, of projects . . . (Sophrony, 1.26.61 HGL 560)

The church, Thomas Merton believed, must contribute to
the forward thrust of humanity. Late in 1961, Merton, writing

as a Christian humanist, wrote of the church's grounding in the incarnation. He noted, therefore, its inherent role as a matrix in advancing the best in humanity, yet he also noted how the ecclesiastical institution can stand in the way of the humanization of persons and cultures. In doing so it may be foreshadowing "the end of Western Christianity."

> What is important is the fully Christian notion of man: a notion radically modified by the mystery of the Incarnation. This I think is the very heart of the matter. And therefore it seems to me that a program of Christian culture needs to be rooted in the biblical notion of man as the object of the divine mercy, of a special concern on the part of God, as the spouse of God, as, in some mysterious sense, an epiphany of the divine wisdom. Man in Christ. The New Adam, presupposing the Old Adam, presupposing the old paradise and the new paradise, the creation and the new creation.
>
> At the present time man has ceased entirely to be seen as any of these. The whole Christian notion of man has turned inside out, instead of paradise we have Auschwitz. . . . [In] Latin Christianity, we come up against a dialectic of fidelity and betrayal, understanding and blindness. That we have come to a certain kind of "end" of the development of Western Christianity is no accident, nor yet is it entirely the responsibility of Christian culture, for Christian culture has precisely saved all that could be saved. Yet was this enough? . . . In a word, perhaps we might profitably run the risk . . . not just of assuming that Christian culture is a body of perfections to be salvaged but of asking where there was infidelity and imperfection. And yet at the same time stressing above all the value and the supreme importance of our Western Christian cultural heritage. For it is the survival of religion as an abstract formality without a humanist matrix, religion apart from man and almost in some sense apart from God Himself (God figuring only as a Lawgiver not as a Saviour), religion without any human epiphany in art, in work, in social forms: . . . God without culture and without humanism tends inevitably to promote a religion that is irreligious and even unconsciously atheistic. (Bruno Schlesinger, 12.13.61 HGL 541–42)

A large part of the problem of the church being true to its spiritual identity lies, as the Trappist saw it, with its over-identification with the secular order. In a letter to social activist and thinker, Gordon Zahn, Merton questioned the relationship of the sacred and the secular.

> We have to face the fact that we have traveled a long way from the real Christian center. Centuries of identification between Christian and civil life have done more to secularize Christianity than to sanctify civil life. This is not a popular idea. I wonder if anyone in our time has really faced it in a satisfactory way without either too much evasion, too total and too oversimpli-fied a rejection of the secular and the temporal, or too complete a submission to it? The problem is enormous . . . (January 1962 HGL 649)

On the eve of Vatican II, Merton expressed his weariness with people's complaints about the church. Yet he realized that the complaints were not without some foundation in reality, as he wrote to Catherine de Hueck Doherty, his friend in New York City who worked with the poor.

> . . . one is tempted to feel he has no right to be weary of the actions and pronouncements of a lot of very good, sincere people who are themselves weary of something or other. We are like a bunch of drunken men at the last end of a long stupid party falling over the furniture in the twilight of dawn. I hope it is dawn. Probably not, though. But the thing that eats one up is the anguish over the Church. . . . there is this conviction that the Church is full of a terrible spiritual sickness, even though there is always that inexpressible life . . .
> . . . What is wanted is love. But love has been buried under words, noise, plans, projects, systems, and apostolic gim-micks. . . . We are afflicted with the disease of constant talking with almost nothing to say. . . . people like to get around the responsibility by entering into a routine of trivialities in which everything seems clear and noble and defined: but when you look at it honestly it falls apart, for it is riddled with absurdity from top to bottom . . . (6.4.62 HGL 19)

The resolution of John Harris's marriage case in Rome drew from the Trappist both a tempered realism as well as a profound faith as he reflected upon the church as the Body of Christ in the summer of 1962. He was, perhaps, remembering his own "blinders" when he jumped into the Bark of Peter in 1938.

> What can I tell you about the Church? . . . In a sense it is true that one only comes in with blinders on, blinders one has put on and kept on. One has to refuse to be disturbed by so many things. And you are right in the refusal. These are temporal and absurd things which, in the eschatological perspectives, which are the true ones, must vanish forever along with many other things that are more precious and far from absurd in themselves.
>
> The Church is not of this world, and she complacently reminds us of this when we try to budge her in any direction. But on the other hand we also are of the Church and we also have our duty to speak up and say the Church is not of this world when her refusal to budge turns out, in effect, to be a refusal to budge from a solidly and immovably temporal position. . . .
>
> . . . You will have the grace to see through all that is inconsequential and unfortunate in the Church. She is still the Church, the Body of Christ, and nobody can change that, not even some of those who imagine themselves to represent her perfectly when they have simply twisted her teachings to suit their own secularism. Be true to the Spirit of God and to Christ. Read your Prophets sometimes, and go through the Gospels and St. Paul and see what is said there: that is your life. You are called to a totally new, risen, transformed life in the Spirit of Christ. A life of simplicity and truth and joy that is not of this world. (Harris, 6.8.62 HGL 398–99)

To convert Jeanne Burdick, Merton wrote of the church as an "ark" into which one scrambles to escape life's flood. As noted earlier, this probably described his own enthusiastic experience of conversion to the church. The monk counseled her to assume her lay responsibilities for the ongoing life of the church, which he refers to for the first time in his published letters as "the people of God"—the image that would later become popular at Vatican II.

The situation in our time is baffling and when one comes into the Church at a time like this one can definitely have the feeling that one is scrambling up the gangplank into the ark. And sometimes one can also be tempted to wonder if the ark itself is going to leak or even founder. But God is the one to worry about that.

If you come into the Church you come with work to do, and you should have a sense that the Catholic laity are an important, very important part of the people of God. The Church is not just an institution for the benefit of priests and nuns, with lay people around to fill in the background. The coming Council may, we hope, give light and direction on these things. (Burdick, 6.11.62 HGL 110)

As Vatican II was about to begin, the Trappist stated his conviction that, despite all of the defects in the institution and its members, the church was nevertheless indefectible because it is of God. He did not speak of the infallibility of the church, however. "The Church is after all a reality, and the central reality: though her members have failed shockingly in their Christian responsibility in many areas, and though there may be a great blindness and weakness pervading whole areas of her life, nevertheless she is indefectible because God lives and acts in her. And this faith must live in us and grow in us, especially when we are tempted against it as we are now" (James Forest, 8.27.62 HGL 270).

A couple weeks later, Thomas Merton expressed those temptations against faith in the church in a letter to philosopher E. I. Watkin. He begins here to speak more urgently of the church being "in crisis."

I cannot say exactly that the Church has given me a bland security in which there is no further sense of isolation. I do not feel snug in her.

As you say, there are many disquieting things to face all around us. And humanly I sometimes wonder if there is any hope of it being otherwise in our lifetime. But it is a time of crisis, a long-overdue crisis, in which the anguish our fathers

did not feel has come upon us, and compounded. I cannot
smugly accept the mere fact of the Church as an institution, as
if this alone were the answer to all problems. An institution
that has held together since the year 33. I doubt if this is a fully
comforting consideration. (9.11.62 HGL 578)

Part of the problem, Merton judged, was the church's continual
complicity with secular interests, for purposes of gain for the
church. ". . . the Church has been too slow to speak and to take
a definite position, and this has been weakness and betrayal
on the part of those whose responsibility it was: they have been
too deeply identified with secular interests" (Doherty, 11.12.62
HGL 20).

Near the end of the first session of Vatican II, the Trappist,
aware that ever more radical reforms were needed in the
church's ways, nevertheless wrote with great faith in the
church's holiness:

> . . . the true reality of the Church is precisely what the Gospel
> said it is: the communion of "saints" in the Holy Spirit. . . .
> (Watkin, 11.15.62 HGL 580)

> . . . I agree with your remarks about the Church. The problem
> is much deeper than many people seem to imagine, though the
> possibilities of renewal, with people like Pope John available,
> are great. Still, I think the approach is not radical enough. Or
> at least, we do not know as yet how radical it is, because for all
> the enthusiasm of some theologians, and I am enthusiastic with
> them, the first session did not really get down to the roots. . . .
> The great problem is the fact that the Church is utterly embed-
> ded in a social matrix that is radically unfriendly to genuine
> spiritual growth because it tends to stifle justice and charity as
> well as genuine inner life. (Watkin, 1.11.63 HGL 581)

To persons of other religious traditions, like the Chinese
scholar John Wu and the Jewish theologian Abraham Heschel,
the Trappist confessed his historical sensitivity to some of the
problems of Western Christianity. To Wu:

Christianity as it has developed in the West, including monasteries of the West, has become a complex and multifarious thing. It takes Chuang Tzu to remind us of an essential element in the Gospel which we have simply "tuned out" . . . And the Discourse of the Last Supper. Even the central message of the Cross and the Resurrection. And the crib full of straw, in which the Lord of the world laughs and says, "You should worry!" (12.20.62 HGL 623)

To Heschel:

We have the bad habit of thinking that because we believe the prophecies are fulfilled, we can consider them to be fulfilled in any way we please, that is to say that we are too confident of understanding this "fulfillment." Consequently, the medieval facility with which the Kingdom of God was assumed to be the society inherited from Charlemagne. And consequently the even more portentous facility with which Christians did exactly what they accused the Jews of having done: finding an earthly fulfillment of prophecy in political institutions dressed up as theocracy.

The twentieth century makes it impossible seriously to do this any more, so perhaps we will be humble enough to dig down to a deeper and more burning truth. In so doing, we may perhaps get closer to you, whom the Lord has not allowed to find so many specious arguments in favor of complacent readings. (1.26.63 HGL 432)

As a monk, Thomas Merton always felt some distance from the issues of ecclesiastical reform. Monastic reform and renewal captured him intensely. But he did not sense that the heated conciliar debates about ecclesiastical reform were such important issues for him personally. The monk stands within but on the margins, even of the church. He disclosed this insider/outsider posture to E. I. Watkin in 1963:

I know exactly how you feel about the Church, and I would say I felt the same way, except that I think I have got to the point where I have not much time to worry about it, and it does not constitute a personal problem. God's will for me is clear enough, and it certainly fits in with His will for the world, whatever that may be. The bishops can take care of themselves, that is their business. (5.7.63 HGL 582)

Merton's comments on the Catholic Church in the United States were neither positive nor optimistic at the beginning of Vatican II. For example, in a letter to his friends in the peace movement, Jean and Hildegard Goss-Mayr, he described what little he knew of the bishops in this country.

> About the American Bishops: I have not much information. Most of them would simply not understand the problem, I am afraid. Archbishop Flahiff of Winnipeg, Canada, is a bright and understanding new bishop . . . Also Bishop Wright of Pittsburgh, very good. Perhaps Cardinal Ritter of St. Louis, who was a pioneer in race relations here. I think he is open-minded. I don't know that there would be much point in seeing the theological advisor of our own Archbishop. This is my friend Msgr. Horrigan, president of a college near here. The Archbishop is too timid and conservative to understand the problem aright, though he is a good man (Archbishop Floersh of Louisville, whom you can see anyway, but don't expect anything much. But he will be delighted you are a friend of mine and will gladly speak to you. I am very fond of him, he ordained me. But he does not see those new issues, I believe. . . .) (10.14.62 HGL 327)

In 1963 the Trappist again expressed his negative views of the Catholic Church in the United States: "I am accused of being very much of a pessimist. But still, those who do so are usually basing their argument on the fact that I don't find much to hope for in the present climate of American Catholicism. This is interpreted by them as a failure of supernatural, theological hope on my part . . ." (Gordon Zahn, 4.30.63 HGL 650).

Merton was particularly critical of the hierarchy in this country with regard to issues of war and peace, as he wrote to social activist James Douglass in 1965:

A Focus on Truth

There is no question at all that some rather representative portions of the U.S. Church have simply identified the Pentagon line with Christianity and are blind to the moral consequences of such an attitude. This is a fact which I can only regard as apocalyptic, much as I hate to be dramatic about it . . .

. . . I am convinced that at the moment the fact that those who protest against total war are regarded as pacifists creates a certain amount of confusion . . . (5.26.65 HGL 160)

In 1967, writing to Dorothy Day, the monk expressed his concern about New York prelate Francis Cardinal Spellman's support of the Vietnam War:

The moral insensitivity of those in authority, on certain points so utterly crucial for man and for the Church, has to be pointed out and if possible dispelled. It does not imply that we ourselves are perfect or infallible. But what is a Church after all but a community in which truth is shared, not a monopoly that dispenses it from the top down. Lights travels on a two-way street in our Church: or I hope it does . . . (2.9.67 HGL 152)

Similar sentiments were written by the Trappist to the Brazilian bishop Dom Helder Camara in the spring of 1967: "I am very much afraid that our bishops here in the United States are dominated by too deep a respect for our government and for our 'establishment' in which as a matter of fact they play a significant part. The inevitable is going to happen and it will be terrifying, for surely judgment will come and it will be painful for the Church" (4.8.67 HGL 111).

Thomas Merton's belief in Christ's church was much deeper than its structures and its rulers. He had experienced the indwelling of the Holy Spirit in the community called church, something that endured no matter what happened to the "skeleton" of the church. Nevertheless, he did express pleasure with the introduction of the conciliar discussion of the collegial governance of the church. "Let's throw out the skeleton for good and all and take off for nowhere with that Vagabond (that notorious illuminist, the Holy Spirit)" (Wu, 6.23.63 HGL 624).

And: "I am very drawn to the Russian idea of *sobornost* [the doctrine of the Spirit acting and leading the whole Church into the truth] which seems to me to be essential to the notion of the Church, in some form or other. I do not know how this can be gainsaid. Collegiality is a step in that direction" (Bolshakoff, 11.11.63 HGL 104).

Too often, in the Trappist's judgment, the church confused her political goals and her mission of salvation, as in the extended and heated debates about conscientious objection to the Vietnam War. This he expressed to Pittsburgh bishop John Wright in 1964: "It seems to me that the Church today faces a great 'temptation' which arises out of the last thousand years or so of her history: that of too closely identifying her policy in affairs of diplomacy etc. with her mission to save souls, and of tending to seek obedience in these matters of policy just as if they did in fact involve the salvation of souls" (1.10.64 HGL 608–9).

In early 1964 Merton's disaffection with the church becomes more evident and dramatic. He confessed to his friend Daniel Berrigan that he often felt alienated from the church. Yet he counseled him not to become frustrated since the Holy Spirit is in charge.

> Even the Church is to some extent its own diaspora. Though the fact that I often feel alien in the Church is no new thing and proves nothing about the Church, I suppose. . . .
>   . . . Do not be discouraged. The Holy Spirit is not asleep. Nor let yourself get too frustrated. There is no use getting mad at the Church and her representatives. . . . God writes straight on crooked lines anyway, all the time, all the time. The lines are crooked enough by now. And we I suppose are what He is writing with, though we can't see what is being written. And what He writes is not for peace of soul, that is sure . . . (2.23.64 HGL 81)

Some of Merton's severest criticisms of the institutional church related to its complicity in the Cold War.

. . . The thing that is worst about the whole involvement of
so-called Christians in the cold war is the way it is assumed
that Christian hope and optimism are built around the survival
of the Church as a plush and privileged establishment in the
affluent society. If this isn't a spiritual apostasy, I'd like to know
what it is. The war theology of the Churches ought to be suf-
ficient demonstration of the fact. (Ferry, 4.4.64 HGL 216)

The summer of 1964 found Merton putting little personal
stock in church reforms, especially in matters related to war
and peace. In a letter to Daniel Berrigan, the Trappist sympathized and identified with the Jesuit's frustrations with the
church in the areas of justice and peace.

It is of course not God's will that a religious or a priest should
spend his life more or less in frustration and defeat over the
most important issues that face the Church. . . . I realize that
I am about at the end of some kind of a line. What line? What
is the trolley I am probably getting off? The trolley is called a
special kind of hope. . . . I don't need to be on the trolley car
anyway, I don't belong riding in a trolley. . . . As a priest I am
a burnt-out case, repeat, burnt-out case. . . . I am waiting to
fall over and it may take about ten more years of writing. When
I fall over, it will be a big laugh because I wasn't there at all.
   . . . where we are all going is where we went a long time
ago, over the falls. We are in a new river and we don't know it.
(8.4.64 HGL 83–84)

As the third session of Vatican II neared, Merton was aware
of the quite different place of the church in the world. The
synthesis of church-world relationship that had existed since
the Middle Ages was clearly over. While he approved of that,
he feared that the church was becoming swallowed up in excessive activism in order to prove that it is still of some value
to—and indeed, even powerful in—the world. This, he judged,
was a betrayal of its purpose as a prayerful and contemplative
presence in the world. He saw some of the latter being better
preserved and expressed in the spirituality of the Church of
England. He wrote to Etta Gullick:

The climate of the Anglican Church seems to me to be quite favorable, especially with the background of the English school. I do honestly feel that the Anglicans have a special job to do, to keep alive this spiritual simplicity and honesty quite apart from all fuss and works. It seems to me that the atmosphere in our Church on the other hand is going to become more and more hostile to contemplative prayer. There will certainly be official pronouncements approving it and blessing it. But in fact the movement points in the direction of activism, and an activistic concept of liturgy. I think the root of the trouble is fear and truculence, unrealized, deep down. The realization that the Church of Rome is not going to be able to maintain a grandiose and preeminent sort of position, the old prestige she has always had and the decisive say in the things of the world, to some extent even in the last centuries. Contemplation will be regarded more and more as an official "dynamo" source of inspiration and power for the big guns out there: Carmelite nuns generating spiritual electricity for the Holy Office, not so much by contemplative prayer as by action and official public prayer within an enclosure.

In a word, the temper of the Roman Church is combative and "aroused" and the emphasis on contemplation is (if there is any at all) dominated by a specific end in view so that implicitly contemplation becomes ordered to action, which is so easy in a certain type of scholastic thought, misunderstood. When this happens, the real purity of the life of prayer is gone. (9.12.64 HGL 367–68)

As the council progressed, Thomas Merton became more and more convinced that the old ways of being church simply had to change. In the middle of Vatican II's third session in 1964 he wrote that too much fixation on past philosophical ways of thinking was making Christianity irrelevant. Interestingly the monk penned these reflections to a Buddhist, Ripu Daman Lama.

It is quite true that Christianity has been slow to abandon philosophical structures which do not have meaning for the man of today. It is even more true that among many Christians there is a lack of a *living* presence and witness to God, but rather an abundance of words and formulas, together with rites that many no longer understand. It is the old problem of institutional religion and of traditions that remain fixed in the past. (11.13.64 HGL 452)

It is often asked whether Merton was a conservative or a progressive, since he frequently showed signs of each. He could not easily be classified in either a political or ideological camp. He remained always a very independent and critical thinker, which often left him standing quite alone. Merton's uncensored expressions about the church in his published letters surely indicate that his "ecclesiology" was idiosyncratic. It was the church of a contemplative who refused to be trapped into any ideological camp. He wrote of this to Islamic Sufi scholar Martin Lings in the spring of 1965:

> Contact with your "school of thought," shall I say, is of great help to me in rectifying my own perspectives in this time when among Catholics one is faced with a choice between an absurdly rigid and baroque conservatism and a rather irresponsible and fantastic progressivism à la Teilhard. The choice is of course not so restricted, and I am glad of influences that help me to cling, as my heart tells me to, to a sane and living traditionalism in full contact with the living contemplative experience of the past—and with the presence of the Spirit here and how. (4.24.65 HGL 454)

The Trappist could be equally as critical of progressives as he could of conservatives.

> To me one of the most amusing things that has happened lately is this: the progressive and activist Catholics began hailing the Beatles as very hip people (which of course they are). Then all of a sudden the Beatles start going to a yogi to learn contemplation—which is anathema to the progressive etc. Catholics. Hm. My feeling is that our progressives don't know what they are talking about, in their declarations about modern man, the

modern world, etc. Perhaps they are dealing with some private myth or other. That is their affair . . . (Bruno Schlesinger, 10.16.67 HGL 546)

In a letter to Vietnamese Buddhist monk Thich Nhat Hanh in June of 1966, Merton expressed his sense that Buddhists and Catholics shared a similar problem of "conservative and formalist religiosity." He believed that "[a] new mentality is needed, and this implies above all a recovery of ancient and original wisdom. And a real contact with what is right before our noses" (6.29.66 HGL 382).

By 1967 Merton's frustration with the church had reached an all-time high. Many of the high hopes for Vatican II reform and renewal seemed to be sidetracked or neglected. After the formal sessions of Vatican II closed in December 1965, the energy dissipated as the Vatican curia attempted to implement the conciliar decrees. As he wrote to Daniel Berrigan in September of 1967: "I'm glad you are at Cornell. It's a good place. Stay away from Catlicks, they are poison" (9.16.67 HGL 96). And in a similar vein, to theologian and social activist James Douglass, Merton wrote: "It is getting clearer and clearer that the institutional Church does not measure up to the tasks that she believes and proclaims to be hers, and it is a wonder more people are not fully aware of that. I guess a lot are . . . (6.30.67 HGL 166).

In a letter to W. H. Ferry, the Trappist expressed his fears that an authoritarian church would destroy itself by becoming increasingly incredible to its thinking members. This, he sensed, is what happened to Fr. Charles Davis, the English theologian, who resigned both the priesthood and his membership in the Roman Catholic Church. Merton was sympathetic, to a point.

A far as I can see, his points are unassailable. Authority has simply been abused too long in the Catholic Church and for many people it just becomes utterly stupid and intolerable to have to put up with the kind of jackassing around that is imposed in God's name. It is an insult to God Himself and in the end it can only discredit all idea of authority and obedience. There comes a point where they simply forfeit the right to be listened to.

On the other hand, I regret that poor [Davis] had to get pushed so far. It doesn't help the rest of us much. If everyone with any sense just pulls out, then that leaves the curial boys in full command of the field with the assurance that they are martyrs to justice or something. The real problem remains the reform of the Church people who remain inside. And if there can only be a little agreement on a more reasonable and free approach, something can be done. With super-organization and overcontrol, the whole works is doomed . . . (1.19.67 HGL 230)

It was in an extensive exchange of views with Rosemary Radford Ruether that the Trappist was most candid about his frustrations and disappointment with institutional Catholicism. Ruether had consulted Merton about how one could be intellectually and spiritually integral and remain active in the Roman Catholic Church. In response Merton expressed his most severe criticisms of institutional Catholicism and his own perceived relationship to it.

In the first month of 1967 the Trappist expressed his doubts and confusions about his own continued belonging to the church. He seemed to be moving to a point similar to that of one of his brothers at Gethsemani Abbey, who told me in the early 1990s: "If I weren't a monk, I could not be a Roman Catholic." Monasticism is and always has been a place within the church yet on the margins of the institution, which allows both personal and even communal divergence and diversity while moving deeper into what church is: a sacrament of the reign of God, but not that reign *in toto*. Church is an instrument of mystery but does not contain the Mystery in an exhaustive way. On the margins, such as in monasticism, one comes to realize that deeper truth.

Merton expressed this view to Ruether with great angst and honesty and humility, in hope that she could help him find where he truly was in the church:

To begin with the Church: I have no problem about "leaving" or anything. My problem with "authority" is just the usual one and I can survive it. But the real Church. I am simply browned off with and afraid of Catholics. All Catholics, from Ottaviani to Du Bay, all down the damn line. There are a few Catholics I can stand with equanimity when I forget they are Catholics, and remember they are just my friends, like Dan Berrigan and Ed Rice and Sister Mary Luke and a lot of people like that. I love the monks but they might as well be in China. I love all the nice well-meaning people who go to Mass and want things to get better and so on, but I understand Zen Buddhists better than I do them and the Zens understand me better. But this is awful because where is the Church and where am I in the Church? You are a person who might have an idea of the Church that might help me and that I might trust. An idea of the Church in which projects and crusades (ancient or modern) or ideas (new or old) or policies or orthodoxies (old or new) don't stand in the way between people. Is the Church a community of people who love each other or a big dogfight where you do your religious business, seeking meanwhile your friends somewhere else?

Could you suggest something good on this? I haven't been reading Catholic stuff, books or magazines, for a long time (except recently Guardini on Pascal). I'd be perfectly content to forget I am a Catholic. I suppose that is bad faith, because meanwhile I continue in a monastery and a hermitage where I am content with life and the institution is supporting me in this . . .

I know this is a pretty bad letter (guilt about saying all this). But I do wonder at times if the Church is real at all. I believe it, you know. But I wonder if I am nuts to do so. Am I part of a great big hoax? I don't explain myself as well as I would like to: there is a real sense of and confidence in an underlying reality, the presence of Christ in the world which I don't doubt for an instant. But is that presence where we are all saying it is? We are all pointing (in various directions) and my dreadful feeling is that we are all pointing wrong. Could you point someplace for me maybe?

. . . I have to write a book on monasticism and I wonder if I can make it relevant—or make any sense with it at all. (I have no problem with my vocation.) (1.29.67 HGL 499–500)

In February 1967 Ruether described the church to be, for her, more "a happening" than an institution. Merton found this shift of image helpful in clarifying his place in or on the margins of the Catholic institution.

> I agree with you all along about the hardening of the Church as institution and idol and its becoming against what it ought to be a sign of. If we and others see this problem—and it is pretty terrible—then there is something going on, anyway, and if there is smoke going up here and there that is something. I also think we will be a very scattered Church for a while. But as long as I know what direction seems to be the one to go in, I will gladly go in it.
>
> So, in your book first of all: what you say about the Church as happening clicks perfectly. I really think what I really wanted to know most of all was that my own personal "sense" of when Church happens was not just self-deception—at least not purely so. Because if that is where God speaks and the Spirit acts, then I can be confident that God has not abandoned us. Not left us at the mercy of the princes of the Church. . . .
>
> . . . What does bother me theologically (I am not enough of a theologian to be really bothered by theological problems) is the sense that, when you go back into the history of the Church, you run into a bigger and bigger hole of unconscious bad faith, and at that point I get rather uneasy about our dictating to all the "other religions" that we are the one authentic outfit that has the real goods. I am not saying that I want to be able to mix Christianity and Buddhism in quantities to suit myself, however. Far from it. I think you got me wrong on that. (2.14.67 HGL 500–501)

Despite what initially seemed to be a renewed sense of place within the institution, Monk Merton, in the following month, found himself wondering if he were not somehow leaving the church without even realizing it. Was the path he was walking simply leading him away from institutional Catholicism? In his continuing search for ecclesial belonging during 1967, the Trappist wrote that perhaps his place was in a different kind of monasticism than he was experiencing at the Abbey of Gethsemani. "Right now I am working on Faulkner, and also writing on Camus, and am, I suppose, again sneaking out the back door of the Church without telling myself that this is what I am doing. I don't feel guilty about this, though, and am conscious of it" (Ruether, 3.24.67 HGL 509).

By mid-1967 Merton had begun to think of himself as somehow post-denominational as he reflected in a letter to Ruether:

> . . . What I do absolutely agree with is the need to be free from a sort of denominational tag. Though I have one in theory (people still have me categorized in terms of The Seven Storey Mtn) I am really not any of the things they think, and I don't comfortably wear the label of monk either, because I am now convinced that the first way to be a decent monk is to be a non-monk and an anti-monk, as far as the "image" goes: but I am certainly quite definite about wanting to stay in the bushes (provided I can make some sort of noises that will reach my offbeat friends) . . . (5.5.67 HGL 511)

Later that same year, however, we find Merton's more hopeful and last recorded published epistolary words about the church. Here the monastic man seems to have come to some accommodation with the limitations of the church because of what he calls "pure faith." As he wrote to Linda Sabbath: "Of all religions, Christianity is the one that least needs techniques, or least needs to depend on them. Nor is the overemphasis on sacraments necessary either: the great thing is faith. With a pure faith, our use of techniques, our understanding of the psyche and our use of the sacraments all become really meaningful. Without it, they are just routines" (8.7.67 HGL 532).

Thomas Merton had written to Catherine de Hueck Doherty in 1966 about what he considered to be the cost of true reform and renewal of the church. Over the years he knew that cost by experience: "Well, we won't really get out of the wilderness until everything is pressed out and there is nothing left but the pure wine to be offered to the Lord, transubstantiated into His Blood" (1.12.66 HGL 24).

Bibliography

Finley, James. *Merton's Palace of Nowhere*. 1978. Notre Dame, IN: Ave Maria Press, 2017.

Hebblethwaite, Peter. *Pope John XXIII: Pope of the Century*. New York: Continuum, 1994.

Merton, Thomas. *Conjectures of a Guilty Bystander*. 1965. New York: Doubleday, 2009.

———. *The Courage for Truth: The Letters of Thomas Merton to Writers*. 1993. Edited by Christine M. Bochen. New York: Farrar, Straus and Giroux, 2011. Kindle.

———. *The Hidden Ground of Love: The Letters of Thomas Merton on Religious Experience and Social Concerns*. 1985. Edited by William H. Shannon. New York: Farrar, Straus and Giroux, 2011. Kindle.

———. *No Man Is an Island* (excerpts). 1955. In *A Thomas Merton Reader*. Edited by Thomas P. McDonnell. New York: Doubleday, 1996.

———. *The Road to Joy: The Letters of Thomas Merton to New and Old Friends*. Edited by Robert E. Daggy. New York: Harcourt Brace Jovanovich, 1989.

———. *The School of Charity: The Letters of Thomas Merton on Religious Renewal and Spiritual Direction*. 1990. Edited by Brother Patrick Hart. New York: Farrar, Straus and Giroux, 2011. Kindle.

———. *The Seven Storey Mountain*. 1948. Orlando, FL: Harcourt, 1999.

———. *A Thomas Merton Reader*. Edited by Thomas P. McDonnell. New York: Doubleday, 1996.

———. *Witness to Freedom: The Letters of Thomas Merton in Times of Crisis.* 1994. Edited by William H. Shannon. New York: Farrar, Straus and Giroux, 2011. Kindle.

Mott, Michael. *The Seven Mountains of Thomas Merton.* Boston: Houghton Mifflin, 1984.

Shannon, William H. *Silent Lamp: The Thomas Merton Story.* New York: Crossroad, 1992.

———. *Thomas Merton's Paradise Journey: Writings on Contemplation.* Cincinnati, OH: St. Anthony Messenger Press, 2000.

Tardiff, Mary, ed. *At Home in the World: The Letters of Thomas Merton and Rosemary Radford Ruether.* Maryknoll, NY: Orbis Books, 1995.